500 Super Easy Homemade Recipes

Linda R. Williams

CORN PUDDING.

This is a Virginia dish. Scrape the substance out of twelve ears of tender, green, uncooked corn (it is better scraped than grated, as you do not get those husky particles which you cannot avoid with a grater); add yolks and whites, beaten separately, of four eggs, a teaspoonful of sugar, the same of flour mixed in a tablespoonful of butter, a small quantity of salt and pepper, and one pint of milk. Bake about half or three-quarters of an hour.

STEWED CORN.

Take a dozen ears of green sweet corn, very tender and juicy; cut off the kernels, cutting with a large sharp knife from the top of the cob down; then scrape the cob. Put the corn in a saucepan over the fire with just enough water to make it cook without burning; boil about twenty minutes, then add a teacupful of milk or cream, a tablespoonful of cold butter, and season with pepper and salt. Boil ten minutes longer and dish up hot in a vegetable dish. The corn would be much sweeter if the scraped cobs were boiled first in the water that the corn is cooked in.

Many like corn cooked in this manner, putting half corn and half tomatoes; either way is very good.

FRIED CORN.

Cut the corn off the cob, taking care not to bring off any of the husk with it and to have the grains as separate as possible. Fry in a little butter—just enough to keep it from sticking to the pan; stir very often. When nicely browned, add salt and pepper and a little rich cream. Do not set it near the stove after the cream is added, as it will be apt to turn. This makes a nice dinner or breakfast dish.

ROASTED GREEN CORN.

Strip off all the husk from green corn and roast it on a gridiron over a bright fire of coals, turning it as one side is done. Or, if a wood fire is used, make a place clean in front of the fire, lay the corn down, turn it when one side is done; serve with salt and butter.

SUCCOTASH.

Take a pint of fresh shelled Lima beans, or any large fresh beans, put them in a pot with cold water, rather more than will cover them. Scrape the kernels from twelve ears of young sweet corn; put the cobs in with the beans, boiling from half to three-quarters of an hour. Now take out the cobs and put in the scraped corn; boil again fifteen minutes, then season with salt and pepper to taste, a piece of butter the size of an egg and half a cup of cream. Serve hot.

FRIED EGG-PLANT.

Take fresh, purple egg-plants of a middling size; cut them in slices a quarter of an inch thick, and soak them for half an hour in cold water, with a teaspoonful of salt in it. Have ready some cracker or bread crumbs and one beaten egg; drain off the water from the slices, lay them on a napkin, dip them in the crumbs and then in the egg, put another coat of crumbs on them and fry them in butter to a light brown. The frying pan must be hot before the slices are put in—they will fry in ten minutes.

You may pare them before you put them into the frying pan, or you may pull off the skins when you take them up. You must not remove them from the water until you are ready to cook them, as the air will turn them black.

STUFFED EGG-PLANT.

Cut the egg-plant in two; scrape out all the inside and put it in a saucepan with a little minced ham; cover with water and boil until soft; drain off the water; add two tablespoonfuls of grated crumbs, a tablespoonful of butter, half a minced onion, salt and pepper; stuff each half of the hull with the mixture; add a small lump of butter to each and bake fifteen minutes. Minced veal or chicken in the place of ham, is equally as good and many prefer it.

STRING BEANS.

Break off the end that grew to the vine, drawing off at the same time the string upon the edge; repeat the same process from the other end; cut them with a sharp knife into pieces half an inch long, and boil them in *just enough* water to *cover* them. They usually require one hour's boiling; but this depends upon their age and freshness. After they have boiled until tender and the water *boiled nearly out*, add pepper and salt, a tablespoonful of butter and a half a cup of cream; if you have not the cream add more butter.

Many prefer to drain them before adding the seasoning; in that case they lose the real goodness of the vegetable.

LIMA AND KIDNEY BEANS.

These beans should be put into boiling water, a little more than enough to cover them, and boiled till tender—from half an hour to two hours; serve with butter and salt upon them.

These beans are in season from the last of July to the last of September. There are several other varieties of beans used as summer vegetables, which are cooked as above.

For Baked Beans, see PORK AND BEANS.

CELERY.

This is stewed the same as green corn, by boiling, adding cream, butter, salt and pepper.

STEWED SALSIFY OR OYSTER-PLANT.

Wash the roots and scrape off their skins, throwing them, as you do so, into cold water, for exposure to the air causes them to immediately turn dark. Then cut crosswise into little thin slices; throw into fresh water, enough to cover; add a little salt and stew in a covered vessel until tender, or about one hour. Pour off a little of the water, add a small lump of butter, a little pepper, and a gill of sweet cream and a teaspoonful of flour stirred to a paste. Boil up and serve hot.

Salsify may be simply boiled and melted butter turned over them.

FRIED SALSIFY.

Stew the salsify as usual till very tender; then with the back of a spoon or a potato jammer mash it very fine. Beat up an egg, add a teacupful of milk, a little flour, butter and seasoning of pepper and salt. Make into little cakes, and fry a light brown in boiling lard.

BEETS BOILED.

Select small-sized, smooth roots. They should be carefully washed, but not cut before boiling, as the juice will escape and the sweetness of the vegetable be impaired, leaving it white and hard. Put them into boiling water, and boil them until tender, which requires often from one to two hours. Do not probe them, but press them with the finger to ascertain if they are sufficiently done. When satisfied of this, take them up, and put them into a pan of cold water, and slip off the outside. Cut them into thin slices, and while hot season with butter, salt, a little pepper and very sharp vinegar.

BAKED BEETS.

Beets retain their sugary, delicate flavor to perfection if they are baked instead of boiled. Turn them frequently while in the oven, using a knife, as the fork allows the juice to run out. When done remove the skin, and serve with butter, salt and pepper on the slices.

STEWED BEETS.

Boil them first and then scrape and slice them. Put them into a stewpan with a piece of butter rolled in flour, some boiled onion and parsley chopped fine, and a little vinegar, salt and pepper. Set the pan on the fire, and let the beets stew for a quarter of an hour.

OKRA.

This grows in the shape of pods, and is of a gelatinous character, much used for soup, and is also pickled; it may be boiled as follows: Put the young and tender pods of long white okra in salted boiling water in granite, porcelain or a tin-lined saucepan—as contact with Iron will discolor it; boil fifteen minutes; remove the stems, and serve with butter, pepper, salt and vinegar if preferred.

ASPARAGUS.

Scrape the stems of the asparagus lightly, but very clean; throw them into cold water and when they are all scraped and very clean, tie them in bunches of equal size; cut the large ends evenly, that the stems may be all of the same length, and put the asparagus into plenty of boiling water, well salted. While it is boiling, cut several slices of bread half an inch thick, pare off the crust and toast it a delicate brown on both sides. When the stalks of the asparagus are tender (it will usually cook in twenty to forty minutes) lift it out directly, or it will lose both its color and flavor and will also be liable to break; dip the toast quickly into the liquor in which it was boiled and dish the vegetable upon it, the heads all lying one way. Pour over white sauce, or melted butter.

ASPARAGUS WITH EGGS.

Boil a bunch of asparagus twenty minutes; cut off the tender tops and lay them in a deep-pie plate, buttering, salting and peppering well. Beat up four eggs, the yolks and whites separately to a stiff froth; add two tablespoonfuls of milk or cream, a tablespoonful of warm butter, pepper and salt to taste. Pour evenly over the asparagus mixture. Bake eight minutes or until the eggs are set. Very good.

GREEN PEAS.

Shell the peas and wash in cold water. Put in boiling water just enough to cover them well and keep them from burning; boil from twenty minutes to half an hour, when the liquor should be nearly boiled out; season with pepper and salt and a good allowance of butter; serve very hot.

This is a very much better way than cooking in a larger quantity of water and draining off the liquor, as that diminishes the sweetness, and much of the fine flavor of the peas is lost. The salt should never be put in the peas before they are tender, unless very young, as it tends to harden them.

STEWED GREEN PEAS.

Into a saucepan of boiling water put two or three pints of young green peas and when nearly done and tender drain in a colander dry; then melt two ounces of butter in two of flour; stir well and boil five minutes longer; should the pods be quite clean and fresh boil them first in the water, remove and put in the peas. The Germans prepare a very palatable dish of sweet young pods alone by simply stirring in a little butter with some savory herbs.

SQUASHES, OR CYMBLINGS.

The green or summer squash is best when the outside is beginning to turn yellow, as it is then less watery and insipid than when younger. Wash them, cut them into pieces and take out the seeds. Boil them about three-quarters of an hour, or till quite tender. When done, drain and squeeze them well till you have pressed out all the water; mash them with a little butter, pepper and salt. Then put the squash thus prepared into a stewpan, set it on hot coals and stir it very frequently till it becomes dry. Take care not to let it burn.

Summer squash is very nice steamed, then prepared the same as boiled.

BOILED WINTER SQUASH.

This is much finer than the summer squash. It is fit to eat in August, and, in a dry warm place, can be kept well all winter. The color is a very bright yellow. Pare it, take out the seeds, cut it in pieces, and stew it slowly till quite soft in a very little water. Afterwards drain, squeeze and press it well; then mash it with a very little butter, pepper and salt. They will boil in from twenty to forty minutes.

BAKED WINTER SQUASH.

Cut open the squash, take out the seeds and without paring cut it up into large pieces; put the pieces on tins or in a dripping-pan, place in a moderately hot oven and bake about an hour. When done, peel and mash like mashed potatoes, or serve the pieces hot on a dish, to be eaten warm with butter like sweet potatoes. It retains its sweetness much better baked this way than when boiled.

VEGETABLE HASH.

Chop rather coarsely the remains of vegetables left from a boiled dinner, such as cabbage, parsnips, potatoes, etc.; sprinkle over them a little pepper, place in a saucepan or frying pan over the fire; put in a piece of butter the size of a hickory nut; when it begins to melt, tip the dish so as to oil the bottom and around the sides; then put in the chopped vegetables, pour in a spoonful or two of hot water from the tea-kettle, cover quickly so as to keep in the steam. When heated thoroughly take off the cover and stir occasionally until well cooked. Serve hot. Persons fond of vegetables will relish this dish very much.

SPINACH.

It should be cooked so as to retain its bright green color and not sent to table, as it so often is, of a dull brown or olive color; to retain its fresh appearance, do not cover the vessel while it is cooking.

Spinach requires close examination and picking, as insects are frequently found among it and it is often gritty. Wash it through three or four waters. Then drain it and put it in boiling water. Fifteen to twenty minutes is generally sufficient time to boil spinach. Be careful to remove the scum. When it is quite tender, take it up, and drain and squeeze it well. Chop it fine, and put it into a saucepan with a piece of butter and a little pepper and salt. Set it on the fire and let it stew five minutes, stirring it all the time, until quite dry. Turn it into a vegetable dish, shape it into a mound, slice some hard-boiled eggs and lay around the top.

GREENS.

About a peck of greens are enough for a mess for a family of six, such as dandelions, cowslips, burdock, chicory and other greens. All greens should be carefully examined, the tough ones thrown out, then be thoroughly washed through several waters until they are entirely free from sand. The addition of a handful of salt to each pan of water used in washing the greens will free them from insects and worms, especially if after the last watering they are allowed to stand in salted water for a half hour or longer. When ready to boil the greens, put them into a large pot half full of boiling water, with a handful of salt, and boil them steadily until the stalks are tender; this will be in from five to twenty minutes, according to the maturity of the greens; but remember that long-continued boiling wastes the tender substances of the leaves, and so diminishes both the bulk and the nourishment of the dish; for this reason it is best to cut away any tough stalks before beginning to cook the greens. As soon as they are tender drain them in a colander, chop them a little and return them to the fire long enough to season them with salt, pepper and butter; vinegar may be added if it is liked; the greens should be served as soon as they are hot.

All kinds of greens can be cooked in this manner.

STEWED CARROTS.

Wash and scrape the carrots and divide them into strips; put them into a stewpan with water enough to cover them; add a spoonful of salt and let them boil slowly until tender; then drain and replace them in the pan, with two tablespoons of butter rolled in flour, shake over a little pepper and salt, then add enough cream or milk to moisten the whole; let it come to a boil and serve hot.

CARROTS MASHED.

Scrape and wash them; cook them tender in boiling water salted slightly. Drain well and mash them. Work in a good piece of butter and season with pepper and salt. Heap up on a vegetable dish and serve hot.

Carrots are also good simply boiled in salted water and dished up hot with melted butter over them.

TURNIPS.

Turnips are boiled plain with or without meat, also mashed like potatoes and stewed like parsnips. They should always be served hot. They require from forty minutes to an hour to cook.

STEWED PUMPKINS.

See stewed pumpkin for pie. Cook the same, then after stewing season the same as mashed potatoes. Pumpkin is good baked in the same manner as baked winter squash.

STEWED ENDIVE.

Ingredients.—Six heads of endive, salt and water, one pint of broth, thickening of butter and flour, one tablespoonful of lemon juice, a small lump of sugar.

Mode.—Wash and free the endive thoroughly from insects, remove the green part of the leaves, and put it into boiling water, slightly salted. Let it remain for ten minutes; then take it out, drain it till there is no water remaining and chop it very fine. Put it into a stewpan with the broth, add a little salt and a lump of sugar, and boil until the endive is perfectly tender. When done, which may be ascertained by squeezing a piece between the thumb and finger, add a thickening of butter and flour and the lemon juice; let the sauce boil up and serve.

Time.—Ten minutes to boil, five minutes to simmer in the broth.

BAKED MUSHROOMS.

Prepare them the same as for stewing. Place them in a baking-pan in a moderate oven. Season with salt, pepper, lemon juice and chopped parsley. Cook in the oven fifteen minutes, baste with butter. Arrange on a dish and pour the gravy over them. Serve with sauce made by heating a cup of cream, two ounces of butter, a tablespoonful of chopped parsley, a little cayenne pepper, salt, a tablespoonful of white sauce and two tablespoonfuls of lemon juice. Put in a saucepan and set on the fire. Stir until thick, but do not let boil. Mushrooms are very nice placed on slices of well-buttered toast when set into the oven to bake. They cook in about fifteen minutes.

STEWED MUSHROOMS.

Time, twenty-one minutes. Button mushrooms, salt to taste, a little butter rolled in flour, two tablespoonfuls of cream or the yolk of one egg. Choose buttons of uniform size. Wipe them clean and white with a wet flannel; put them in a stewpan with a little water and let them stew very gently for a quarter of an hour. Add salt to taste, work in a little flour and butter, to make the liquor about as thick as cream, and let it boil for five minutes. When you are ready to dish it up, stir in two tablespoonfuls of cream or the yolk of an egg; stir it over the fire for a minute, but do not let it boil, and serve. Stewed button mushrooms are very nice, either in fish stews or ragouts, or served apart to eat with fish. Another way of doing them is to stew them in milk and water (after they are rubbed white), add to them a little veal gravy, mace and salt and thicken the gravy with cream or the yolks of eggs.

Mushrooms can be cooked in the same manner as the recipes for oysters, either stewed, fried, broiled, or as a soup. They are also used to flavor sauces, catsups, meat gravies, game and soups.

CANNED MUSHROOMS.

Canned mushrooms may be served with good effect with game and even with beefsteak if prepared in this way: Open the can and pour off every drop of the liquid found there; let the mushrooms drain, then put them in a saucepan with a little cream and butter, pepper and salt; let them simmer gently for from five to ten minutes, and when the meat is on the platter pour the mushrooms over it. If served with steak, that should be very tender and be broiled, never in any case fried.

MUSHROOMS FOR WINTER USE.

Wash and wipe free from grit the small fresh button mushrooms. Put into a frying pan a quarter of a pound of the very best butter. Add to it two whole cloves, a saltspoonful of salt and a tablespoonful of lemon juice. When hot add a quart of the small mushrooms, toss them about in the butter for a moment only, then put them in jars; fill the top of each jar with an inch or two of the butter and let it cool. Keep the jars in a cool place, and when the butter is quite firm add a top layer of salt. Cover to keep out dust.

The best mushrooms grow on uplands or in high open fields, where the air is pure.

TRUFFLES.

The truffle belongs to the family of the mushrooms; they are used principally in this country as a condiment for boned turkey and chicken, scrambled eggs, fillets of beef, game and fish. When mixed in due proportion, they add a peculiar zest and flavor to sauces that cannot be found in any other plant in the vegetable kingdom.

ITALIAN STYLE OF DRESSING TRUFFLES.

Ten truffles, a quarter of a pint of salad oil, pepper and salt to taste, one tablespoonful of minced parsley, a very little finely minced garlic, two blades of pounded mace, one tablespoonful of lemon juice.

After cleansing and brushing the truffles, cut them into thin slices and put them in a baking-dish, on a seasoning of oil or butter, pepper, salt, parsley, garlic and mace in the above proportion. Bake them for nearly an hour, and just before serving add the lemon juice and send them to the table very hot.

TRUFFLES AU NATUREL.

Select some fine truffles; cleanse them by washing them in several waters with a brush until not a particle of sand or grit remains on them; wrap each truffle in buttered paper and bake in a hot oven for quite an hour; take off the paper; wipe the truffles and serve them in a hot napkin.

MACARONI.

MACARONI Á LA ITALIENNE.

Divide a quarter of a pound of macaroni into four-inch pieces. Simmer fifteen minutes in plenty of boiling water, salted. Drain. Put the macaroni into a saucepan and turn over it a strong soup stock, enough to prevent burning. Strew over it an ounce of grated cheese; when the cheese is melted, dish. Put alternate layers of macaroni and cheese, then turn over the soup stock and bake half an hour.

MACARONI AND CHEESE.

Break half a pound of macaroni into pieces an inch or two long; cook it in boiling water, enough to cover it well; put in a good teaspoonful of salt; let it boil about twenty minutes. Drain it well and then put a layer in the bottom of a well-buttered pudding-dish; upon this some grated cheese and small pieces of butter, a bit of salt, then more macaroni, and so on, filling the dish; sprinkle the top layer with a thick layer of cracker crumbs. Pour over the whole a teacupful of cream or milk. Set it in the oven and bake half an hour. It should be nicely browned on top. Serve in the same dish in which it was baked with a clean napkin pinned around it.

TIMBALE OF MACARONI.

Break in very short lengths small macaroni (vermicelli, spaghetti, tagliarini). Let it be rather overdone; dress it with butter and grated cheese; then work into it one or two eggs, according to quantity. Butter and bread crumb a plain mold, and when the macaroni is nearly cold fill the mold with it, pressing it well down and leaving a hollow in the centre, into which place a well-flavored mince of meat, poultry or game; then fill up the mold with more macaroni, pressed well down. Bake in a moderately heated oven, turn out and serve.

MACARONI Á LA CRÊME.

Boil one-quarter of a pound of macaroni in plenty of hot water, salted, until tender; put half a pint of milk in a double boiler, and when it boils stir into it a mixture of two tablespoonfuls of butter and one of flour. Add two tablespoonfuls of cream, a little white and cayenne pepper; salt to taste, and from one-quarter to one-half a pound of grated cheese, according to taste. Drain and dish the macaroni; pour the boiling sauce over it and serve immediately.

MACARONI AND TOMATO SAUCE.

Divide half a pound of macaroni into four-inch pieces, put it into boiling salted water enough to cover it; boil from fifteen to twenty minutes then drain; arrange it neatly on a hot dish and pour tomato sauce over it, and serve immediately while hot. See SAUCES for tomato sauce.

BUTTER AND CHEESE

TO MAKE BUTTER.

Thoroughly scald the churn, then cool well with ice or spring water. Now pour in the thick cream; churn fast at first, then, as the butter forms, more slowly; always with perfect regularity; in warm weather, pour a little cold water into the churn, should the butter form slowly; in the winter, if the cream is too cold, add a little warm water to bring it to the proper temperature. When the butter has "come", rinse the sides of the churn down with cold water and take the butter up with a perforated dasher or a wooden ladle, turning it dexterously just below the surface of the buttermilk to catch every stray bit; have ready some very cold water in a deep wooden tray; and into this plunge the dasher when you draw it from the churn; the butter will float off, leaving the dasher free. When you have collected all the butter, gather behind a wooden butter ladle and drain off the water, squeezing and pressing the butter with the ladle; then pour on more cold water and work the butter with the ladle to get the milk out, drain off the water, sprinkle salt over the butter—a tablespoonful to a pound; work it in a little and set in a cool place for an hour to harden, then work and knead it until not another drop of water exudes, and the butter is perfectly smooth, and close in texture and polish; then with the ladle make up into rolls, little balls, stamped pats, etc.

The churn, dasher, tray and ladle should be well scalded before using, so that the butter will not stick to them, and then cooled with very cold water.

When you skim cream into your cream jar, stir it well into what is already there, so that it may all sour alike; and no *fresh cream should be put with it* within twelve hours before churning, or the butter will not come quickly; and perhaps, not at all.

Butter is indispensable in almost all culinary preparations. Good fresh butter, used in moderation, is easily digested; it is softening, nutritious and fattening, and is far more easily digested than any other of the oleaginous substances sometimes used in its place.

TO MAKE BUTTER QUICKLY.

Immediately after the cow is milked, strain the milk into clean pans, and set it over a moderate fire until it is scalding hot; do not let it boil; then set it aside; when it is cold, skim off the cream; the milk will still be fit for any ordinary use; when you have enough cream put it into a clean earthen basin; beat it with a wooden spoon until the butter is made, which will not be long; then take it from the milk and work it with a little cold water, until it is free from milk; then drain off the water, put a small tablespoonful of fine salt to each pound of butter and work it in. A small teaspoonful of fine white sugar, worked in with the salt, will be found an improvement—sugar is a great preservative. Make the butter in a roll; cover it with a bit of muslin and keep it in a cool place. A reliable recipe.

A BRINE TO PRESERVE BUTTER.

First work your butter into small rolls, wrapping each one carefully in a clean muslin cloth, tying them up with a string. Make a brine, say three gallons, having it strong enough of salt to bear up an egg; add half a teacupful of pure, white sugar, and one tablespoonful of saltpetre; boil the brine, and when cold strain it carefully. Pour it over the rolls so as to more than cover them, as this excludes the air. Place a weight over all to keep the rolls under the surface.

PUTTING UP BUTTER TO KEEP.

Take of the best pure common salt two quarts, one ounce of white sugar and one of saltpetre; pulverize them together completely. Work the butter well, then thoroughly work in an ounce of this mixture to every pound of butter. The butter is to be made into half-pound rolls, and put into the following brine—to three gallons of brine strong enough to bear an egg, add a quarter of a pound of white sugar.

CURDS AND CREAM.

One gallon of milk will make a moderate dish. Put one spoonful of prepared rennet to each quart of milk, and when you find that it has become curd, tie it loosely in a thin cloth and hang it to drain; do not wring or press the cloth; when drained, put the curd into a mug and set in cool water, which must be frequently changed (a refrigerator saves this trouble). When you dish it, if there is whey in the mug, lie it gently out without pressing the curd; lay it on a deep dish, and pour fresh cream over it; have powdered loaf-sugar to eat with it; also hand the nutmeg grater.

Prepared rennet can be had at almost any druggist's, and at a reasonable price.

NEW JERSEY CREAM CHEESE.

First scald the quantity of milk desired; let it cool a little, then add the rennet; the directions for quantity are given on the packages of "Prepared Rennet." When the curd is formed, take it out on a ladle without breaking it; lay it on a thin cloth held by two persons; dash a ladleful of water over each ladleful of curd, to separate the curd; hang it up to drain the water off, and then put it under a light press for one hour; cut the curd with a thread into small pieces; lay a cloth between each two, and press for an hour; take them out, rub them with fine salt, let them lie on a board for an hour, and wash them in cold water; let them lie to drain, and in a day or two the skin will look dry; put some sweet grass under and over them, and they will soon ripen.

COTTAGE CHEESE.

Put a pan of sour or loppered milk on the stove or range where it is not too hot; let it scald until the whey rises to the top (be careful that it does not boil, or the curd will become hard and tough). Place a clean cloth or towel over a sieve and pour this whey and curd into it, living it covered to drain two or three hours; then put it into a dish and chop it fine with a spoon, adding a teaspoonful of salt, a tablespoonful of butter and enough sweet cream to make the cheese the consistency of putty. With your hands make it into little balls flattened. Keep it in a cool place. Many like it made rather thin with cream, serving it in a deep dish. You may make this cheese of sweet milk by forming the curd with prepared rennet.

SLIP.

Slip is bonny-clabber without its acidity, and so delicate is its flavor that many persons like it just as well as ice cream. It is prepared thus:—Make a quart of milk moderately warm; then stir into it one large spoonful of the preparation called rennet; set it by, and when cool again it will be as stiff as jelly. It should be made only a few hours before it is to be used, or it will be tough and watery; in summer set the dish on ice after it has jellied. It must be served with powdered sugar, nutmeg and cream.

CHEESE FONDU.

Melt an ounce of butter and whisk into it a pint of boiled milk. Dissolve two tablespoonfuls of flour in a gill of cold milk, add it to the boiled milk and let it cool. Beat the yolks of four eggs with a heaping teaspoonful of salt, half a teaspoonful of pepper and five ounces of grated cheese. Whip the whites of the eggs and add them, pour the mixture into a deep tin lined with buttered paper, and allow for the rising, say four inches. Bake twenty minutes and serve the moment it leaves the oven.

CHEESE SOUFFLÉ.

Melt an ounce of butter in a saucepan; mix smoothly with it one ounce of flour, a pinch of salt and cayenne and a quarter of a pint of milk; simmer the mixture gently over the fire, stirring it all the time, till it is as thick as melted butter, stir into it about three ounces of finely-grated parmesan, or any good cheese. Turn it into a basin and mix with it the yolks of two well-beaten eggs. Whisk three whites to a solid froth, and just before the souffle is baked put them into it, and pour the mixture into a small round tin. It should be only half filled, as the fondu will rise very high. Pin a napkin around the dish in which it is baked, and serve the moment it is baked. It would be well to have a metal cover strongly heated. Time twenty minutes. Sufficient for six persons.

SCALLOPED CHEESE.

Any person who is fond of cheese could not fail to favor this recipe.

Take three slices of bread well-buttered, first cutting off the brown outside crust. Grate fine a quarter of a pound of any kind of good cheese; lay the bread in layers in a buttered baking-dish, sprinkle over it the grated cheese, some salt and pepper to taste. Mix four well-beaten eggs with three cups of milk; pour it over the bread and cheese. Bake it in a hot oven as you would cook a bread pudding. This makes an ample dish for four people.

PASTRY RAMAKINS.

Take the remains or odd pieces of any light puff paste left from pies or tarts; gather up the pieces of paste, roll it out evenly, and sprinkle it with grated cheese of a nice flavor. Fold the paste in three, roll it out again, and sprinkle more cheese over; fold the paste, roll it out, and with a paste-cutter shape it in any way that may be desired. Bake the ramakins in a brisk oven from ten to fifteen minutes; dish them on a hot napkin and serve quickly. The appearance of this dish may be very much improved by brushing the ramakins over with yolk of egg before they are placed in the oven. Where expense is not objected to, parmesan is the best kind of cheese to use for making this dish.

Very nice with a cup of coffee for a lunch.

CAYENNE CHEESE STRAWS.

A quarter of a pound of flour, two ounces butter, two ounces grated parmesan cheese, a pinch of salt and a few grains of cayenne pepper. Mix into a paste with the yolk of an egg. Roll out to the thickness of a silver quarter, about four or five inches long; cut into strips about a third of an inch wide, twist them as you would a paper spill and lay them on a baking-sheet slightly floured. Bake in a moderate oven until crisp, but they must not be the least brown. If put away in a tin these straws will keep a long time. Serve cold, piled tastefully on a glass dish. You can make the straws of remnants of puff pastry, rolling in the grated cheese.

CHEESE CREAM TOAST.

Stale bread may be served as follows: Toast the slices and cover them slightly with grated cheese; make a cream for ten slices out of a pint of milk and two tablespoonfuls of plain flour. The milk should be boiling, and the flour mixed in a little cold water before stirring in. When the cream is nicely cooked, season with salt and butter; set the toast and cheese in the oven for three or four minutes and then pour the cream over them.

WELSH RAREBIT.

Grate three ounces of dry cheese and mix it with the yolks of two eggs, put four ounces of grated bread and three of butter; beat the whole together in a mortar with a dessertspoonful of made mustard, a little salt and some pepper; toast some slices of bread, cut off the outside crust, cut it in shapes and spread the paste thick upon them, and put them in the oven, let them become hot and slightly browned, serve hot as possible.

EGGS AND OMELETS.

There are so many ways of cooking and dressing eggs, that it seems unnecessary for the ordinary family to use those that are not the most practical.

To ascertain the freshness of an egg, hold it between your thumb and forefinger in a horizontal position, with a strong light in front of you. The fresh egg will have a clear appearance, both upper and lower sides being the same. The stale egg will have a clear appearance at the lower side, while the upper side will exhibit a dark or cloudy appearance.

Another test is to put them in a pan of cold water; those that are the first to sink are the freshest; the stale will rise and float on top; or, if the large end turns up in the water, they are not fresh. The best time for preserving eggs is from July to September.

TO PRESERVE EGGS.

There are several recipes for preserving eggs and we give first one which we know to be effectual, keeping them fresh from August until Spring. Take a piece of quick-lime as large as a good-sized lemon and two teacupfuls of salt; put it into a large vessel and slack it with a gallon of boiling water. It will boil and bubble until thick as cream; when it is cold, pour off the top, which will be perfectly clear. Drain off this liquor, and pour it over your eggs; see that the liquor more than covers them. A stone jar is the most convenient—one that holds about six quarts.

Another manner of preserving eggs is to pack them in a jar with layers of salt between, the large end of the egg downward, with a thick layer of salt at the top; cover tightly and set in a cool place.

Some put them in a wire basket or a piece of mosquito net and dip them in boiling water half a minute; then pack in sawdust. Still another manner is to dissolve a cheap article of gum arabic, about as thin as muscilage, and brush over each egg with it; then pack in powdered charcoal; set in a cool, dark place.

Eggs can be kept for some time by smearing the shells with butter or lard; then packed in plenty of bran or sawdust, the eggs not allowed to touch one another; or coat the eggs with melted paraffine.

BOILED EGGS.

Eggs for boiling cannot be too fresh, or boiled too soon after they are laid; but rather a longer time should be allowed for boiling a new-laid egg than for one that is three or four days old. Have ready a saucepan of boiling water; put the eggs into it gently with a spoon, letting the spoon touch the bottom of the saucepan before it is withdrawn, that the egg may not fall and consequently crack. For those who like eggs lightly boiled, three minutes will be found sufficient; three and three-quarters to four minutes will be ample time to set the white nicely; and if liked hard, six or seven minutes will not be found too long. Should the eggs be unusually large, as those of black Spanish fowls sometimes are, allow an extra half minute for them. Eggs for salad should be boiled for ten or fifteen minutes, and should be placed in a basin of cold water for a few minutes to shrink the meat from the shell; they should then be rolled on the table with the hand and the shell will peel off easily.

SOFT BOILED EGGS.

When properly cooked eggs are done evenly through, like any other food. This result may be obtained by putting the eggs into a dish with a cover, or a tin pail, and then pouring upon them *boiling* water—two quarts or more to a dozen of eggs—and cover and set them away where they will keep *hot* and *not* boil for ten to twelve minutes. The heat of the water cooks the eggs slowly, evenly and sufficiently, leaving the centre or yolk harder than the white, and the egg tastes as much richer and nicer as a fresh egg is nicer than a stale egg.

SCALLOPED EGGS.

Hard-boil twelve eggs; slice them thin in rings; in the bottom of a large well-buttered baking-dish place a layer of grated bread crumbs, then one of eggs; cover with bits of butter and sprinkle with pepper and salt. Continue thus to blend these ingredients until the dish is full; be sure, though, that the crumbs cover the eggs upon top. Over the whole pour a large teacupful of sweet cream or milk and brown nicely in a moderately heated oven.

SHIRRED EGGS.

Set into the oven until quite hot a common white dish large enough to hold the number of eggs to be cooked, allowing plenty of room for each. Melt in it a small piece of butter, and breaking the eggs carefully in a saucer, one at a time, slip them into the hot dish; sprinkle over them a small quantity of pepper and salt and allow them to cook four or five minutes. Adding a tablespoonful of cream for every two eggs, when the eggs are first slipped in, is a great improvement.

This is far more delicate than fried eggs.

Or prepare the eggs the same and set them in a steamer over boiling water.

They are usually served in hotels baked in individual dishes, about two in a dish, and in the same dish they were baked in.

SCRAMBLED EGGS.

Put a tablespoonful of butter into a hot frying pan; tip around so that it will touch all sides of the pan. Having ready half a dozen eggs broken in a dish, salted and peppered, turn them (without beating) into the hot butter; stir them one way briskly for five or six minutes or until they are mixed. Be careful that they do not get too hard. Turn over toast or dish up without.

POACHED OR DROPPED EGGS.

Have one quart of *boiling* water and one tablespoonful of salt in a frying pan. Break the eggs, one by one, into a saucer, and slide carefully into the salted water. Dash with a spoon a little water over the egg, to keep the top white.

The beauty of a poached egg is for the yolk to be seen blushing through the white, which should only be just sufficiently hardened to form a transparent veil for the egg.

Cook until the white is firm, and lift out with a griddle cake turner and place on toasted bread. Serve immediately.

A tablespoonful of vinegar put into the water keeps the eggs from spreading.

Open gem rings are nice placed in the water and an egg dropped into each ring.

FRIED EGGS.

Break the eggs, one at a time, into a saucer, and then slide them carefully off into a frying pan of lard and butter mixed, dipping over the eggs the hot grease in spoonfuls, or turn them over, frying both sides without breaking them. They require about three minutes' cooking.

Eggs can be fried round like balls, by dropping one at a time into a quantity of hot lard, the same as for fried cakes, first stirring the hot lard with a stick until it runs round like a whirlpool; this will make the eggs look like balls. Take out with a skimmer. Eggs can be poached the same in boiling water.

EGGS AUX FINES HERBES.

Roll an ounce of butter in a good teaspoonful of flour; season with pepper, salt and nutmeg; put it into a coffeecupful of fresh milk, together with two teaspoonfuls of chopped parsley; stir and simmer it for fifteen minutes, add a teacupful of thick cream. Hard-boil five eggs and halve them; arrange them in a dish with the ends upwards, pour the sauce over them, and decorate with little heaps of fried bread crumbs round the margin of the dish.

POACHED EGGS Á LA CRÊME.

Put a quart of hot water, a tablespoonful of vinegar and a teaspoonful of salt into a frying pan, and break each egg separately into a saucer; slip the egg carefully into the hot water, simmer three or four minutes until the white is set, then with a skimmer lift them out into a hot dish. Empty the pan of its contents, put in half a cup of cream, or rich milk; if milk, a large spoonful of butter; pepper and salt to taste, thicken with a very little cornstarch; let it boil up once, and turn it over the dish of poached eggs. It can be served on toast or without.

It is a better plan to warm the cream in butter in a separate dish, that the eggs may not have to stand.

EGGS IN CASES.

Make little paper cases of buttered writing paper; put a small piece of butter in each, and a little chopped parsley or onion, pepper and salt. Place the cases upon a gridiron over a moderate fire of bright coals, and when the butter melts, break a fresh egg into each case. Strew in upon them a few seasoned bread crumbs, and when nearly done, glaze the tops with a hot shovel. Serve in the paper cases.

MINCED EGGS.

Chop up four or five hard-boiled eggs; do not mince them too fine. Put over the fire in a suitable dish a cupful of milk, a tablespoonful of butter, salt and pepper, and some savory chopped small. When this comes to a boil stir into it a tablespoonful of flour, dissolved in a little cold milk. When it cooks thick like cream put in the minced eggs. Stir it gently around and around for a few moments and serve, garnished with sippets of toast. Any particular flavor may be given to this dish, such as that of mushrooms, truffles, catsup, essence of shrimps, etc., or some shred anchovy may be added to the mince.

MIXED EGGS AND BACON.

Take a nice rasher of mild bacon; cut it into squares no larger than dice; fry it quickly until nicely browned; but on no account burn it. Break half a dozen eggs into a basin, strain and season them with pepper, add them to the bacon, stir the whole about and, when sufficiently firm, turn it out into a dish. Decorate with hot pickles.

MIXED EGGS GENERALLY—SAVORY OR SWEET.

Much the same method is followed in mixed eggs generally, whatever may be added to them; really it is nothing more than an omelet which is stirred about in the pan while it is being dressed, instead of being allowed to set as a pancake. Chopped tongue, oysters, shrimps, sardines, dried salmon, anchovies, herbs, may be used.

COLD EGGS FOR A PICNIC.

This novel way of preparing cold egg for the lunch-basket fully repays one for the extra time required. Boil hard several eggs, halve them lengthwise; remove the yolks and chop them fine with cold chicken, lamb, veal or any tender, roasted meat; or with bread soaked in milk and any salad, as parsley, onion, celery, the bread being half of the whole; or with grated cheese, a little olive oil, drawn butter, flavored. Fill the cavity in the egg with either of these mixtures, or any similar preparation. Press the halves together, roll twice in beaten egg and bread crumbs, and dip into boiling lard. When the color rises delicately, drain them and they are ready for use.

OMELETS.

In making an omelet, care should be taken that the omelet pan is hot and dry. To insure this, put a small quantity of lard or suet into a clean frying pan, let it simmer a few minutes, then remove it; wipe the pan dry with a towel, and then put in a tablespoonful of butter. The smoothness of the pan is most essential, as the least particle of roughness will cause the omelet to stick. As a general rule, a small omelet can be made more successfully than a large one, it being much better to make two small ones of four eggs each, than to try double the number of eggs in one omelet and fail. Allow one egg to a person in making an omelet and one tablespoonful of milk; this makes an omelet more puffy and tender than one made without milk. Many prefer them without milk.

Omelets are called by the name of what is added to give them flavor, as minced ham, salmon, onions, oysters, etc., beaten up in the eggs in due quantity, which gives as many different kind of omelets.

They are also served over many kinds of thick sauces or purees, such as tomato, spinach, endive, lettuce, celery, etc.

If vegetables are to be added, they should be already cooked, seasoned and hot; place in the centre of the omelet, just before turning; so with mushroom, shrimps, or any cooked ingredients. All omelets should be served the moment they are done, as they harden by standing, and care taken that they do not *cook too much*.

Sweet omelets are generally used for breakfast or plain desserts.

PLAIN OMELET.

Put a smooth, clean, iron frying pan on the fire to heat; meanwhile, beat four eggs very light, the whites to a stiff froth and the yolks to a thick batter. Add to the yolks four tablespoonfuls of milk, pepper and salt; and, lastly, stir in the whites lightly. Put a piece of butter nearly half the size of an egg into the heated pan; turn it so that it will moisten the entire bottom, taking care that it does not scorch. Just as it begins to boil, pour in the eggs. Hold the frying pan handle in your left hand, and, as the eggs whiten, carefully, with a spoon, draw up lightly from the bottom, letting the raw part run out on the pan, till all be equally cooked; shake with your left hand, till the omelet be free from the pan, then turn with a spoon one half of the omelet over the other; let it remain a moment, but continue shaking, lest it adhere; toss to a warm platter held in the right hand, or lift with a flat, broad shovel; the omelet will be firm around the edge, but creamy and light inside.

MEAT OR FISH OMELETS.

Take cold meat, fish, game or poultry of any kind; remove all skin, sinew, etc., and either cut it small or pound it to a paste in a mortar, together with a proper proportion of spices and salt; then either toss it in a buttered frying pan over a clear fire till it begins to brown and pour beaten eggs upon it, or beat it up with the eggs, or spread it upon them after they have begun to set in the pan. In any case serve hot, with or without a sauce, but garnish with crisp herbs in branches, pickles, or sliced lemon. The right proportion is one tablespoonful of meat to four eggs. A little milk, gravy, water, or white wine, may be advantageously added to the eggs while they are being beaten.

Potted meats make admirable omelets in the above manner.

VEGETABLE OMELET.

Make a purée by mashing up ready-dressed vegetables, together with a little milk, cream or gravy and some seasoning. The most suitable vegetables are cucumbers, artichokes, onions, sorrel, green peas, tomatoes, lentils, mushrooms, asparagus tops, potatoes, truffles or turnips. Prepare some eggs by beating them very light. Pour them into a nice hot frying pan, containing a spoonful of butter; spread the purée upon the upper side; and when perfectly hot, turn or fold the omelet together and serve. Or cold vegetables may be merely chopped small, then tossed in a little butter, and some beaten and seasoned eggs poured over.

OMELET OF HERBS.

Parsley, thyme and sweet marjoram mixed gives the famous *omelette aux fines herbes* so popular at every wayside inn in the most remote corner of sunny France. An omelet "jardiniere" is two tablespoonfuls of mixed parsley, onion, chives, shallots and a few leaves each of sorrel and chevril, minced fine and stirred into the beaten eggs before cooking. It will take a little more butter to fry it than a plain one.

CHEESE OMELET.

Beat up three eggs, and add to them a tablespoonful of milk and a tablespoonful of grated cheese; add a little more cheese before folding; turn it out on a hot dish; grate a little cheese over it before serving.

ASPARAGUS OMELET.

Boil with a little salt, and until about half cooked, eight or ten stalks of asparagus, and cut the eatable part into rather small pieces; beat the egg and mix the asparagus with them. Make the omelet as above directed. Omelet with parsley is made by adding a little chopped parsley.

TOMATO OMELET. No. 1.

Peel a couple of tomatoes, which split into four pieces; remove the seeds and cut them into small dice; then fry them with a little butter until nearly done, adding salt and pepper. Beat the eggs and mix the tomatoes with them, and make the omelet as usual. Or stew a few tomatoes in the usual way and spread over before folding.

TOMATO OMELET. No. 2.

Cut in slices and place in a stewpan six peeled tomatoes; add a tablespoonful of cold water, a little pepper and salt. When they begin to simmer, break in six eggs, stir well, stirring one way, until the eggs are cooked, but not too hard. Serve warm.

RICE OMELET.

Take a cup of cold boiled rice, turn over it a cupful of warm milk, add a tablespoonful of butter melted, a level teaspoonful of salt, a dash of pepper; mix well, then add three well-beaten eggs. Put a tablespoonful of butter in a hot frying pan, and when it begins to boil pour in the omelet and set the pan in a hot oven. As soon as it is cooked through, fold it double, turn it out on a hot dish, and serve at once. Very good.

HAM OMELET.

Cut raw ham into dice, fry with butter and when cooked enough, turn the beaten egg over it and cook as a plain omelet.

If boiled ham is used, mince it and mix with the egg after they are beaten. Bacon may be used instead of raw ham.

CHICKEN OMELET.

Mince rather fine one cupful of cooked chicken, warm in a teacupful of cream or rich milk a tablespoonful of butter, salt and pepper; thicken with a large tablespoonful of flour. Make a plain omelet, then add this mixture just before turning it over. This is much better than the dry minced chicken. Tongue is equally good.

MUSHROOM OMELET.

Clean a cupful of large button mushrooms, canned ones may be used; cut them into bits. Put into a stewpan an ounce of butter and let it melt; add the mushrooms, a teaspoonful of salt, half a teaspoonful of pepper and half a cupful of cream or milk. Stir in a teaspoonful of flour, dissolved in a little milk or water to thicken, if needed. Boil ten minutes, and set aside until the omelet is ready.

Make a plain omelet the usual way, and just before doubling it, turn the mushrooms over the centre and serve hot.

OYSTER OMELET.

Parboil a dozen oysters in their own liquor, skim them out and let them cool; add them to the beaten eggs, either whole or minced. Cook the same as a plain omelet.

Thicken the liquid with butter rolled in flour; season with salt, cayenne pepper and a teaspoonful of chopped parsley. Chop up the oysters and add to the sauce. Put a few spoonfuls in the centre of the omelet before folding; when dished, pour the remainder of the sauce around it.

FISH OMELET.

Make a plain omelet, and when ready to fold, spread over it fish prepared as follows: Add to a cupful of any kind of cold fish, broken fine, cream enough to moisten it, seasoned with a tablespoonful of butter; then pepper and salt to taste. Warm together.

ONION OMELET.

Make a plain omelet, and when ready to turn spread over it a teaspoonful each of chopped onion and minced parsley; then fold, or, if preferred, mix the minces into the eggs before cooking.

JELLY OMELET.

Make a plain omelet, and just before folding together, spread with some kind of jelly. Turn out on a warm platter. Dust it with powdered sugar.

BREAD OMELET. No. 1.

Break four eggs into a basin and carefully remove the treadles; have ready a tablespoonful of grated and sifted bread; soak it in either milk, water, cream, white wine, gravy, lemon juice, brandy or rum, according as the omelet is intended to be sweet or savory. Well beat the eggs together with a little nutmeg, pepper and salt; add the bread, and, beating constantly (or the omelet will be crumbly), get ready a frying pan, buttered and made thoroughly hot; put in the omelet; do it on one side only; turn it upon a dish, and fold it double to prevent the steam from condensing. Stale sponge-cake, grated biscuit, or pound cake, may replace the bread for a sweet omelet, when pounded loaf sugar should be sifted over it, and the dish decorated with lumps of currant jelly. This makes a nice dessert.

BREAD OMELET. No. 2.

Let one teacupful of milk come to a boil, pour it over one teacupful of bread crumbs and let it stand a few minutes. Break six eggs into a bowl, stir (not beat) till well mixed; then add the milk and bread, season with pepper and salt, mix all well together and turn into a hot frying pan, containing a large spoonful of butter boiling hot. Fry the omelet slowly, and when brown on the bottom cut in squares and turn again, fry to a delicate brown and serve hot.

Cracker omelet may be made by substituting three or four rolled crackers in place of bread.

BAKED OMELET.

Beat the whites and yolks of four or six eggs separately; add to the yolks a small cup of milk, a tablespoonful of flour or cornstarch, a teaspoonful of baking powder, one-half teaspoonful of salt, and, lastly, the stiff-beaten whites. Bake in a well-buttered pie-tin or plate about half an hour in a steady oven. It should be served the moment it is taken from the oven, as it is liable to fall.

OMELET SOUFFLÉ.

Break six eggs into separate cups; beat four of the yolks, mix with them one teaspoonful of flour, three tablespoonfuls of powdered sugar, very little salt. Flavor with extract lemon or any other of the flavors that may be preferred. Whisk the whites of six eggs to a firm froth; mix them lightly with the yolks; pour the mixture into a greased pan or dish; bake in a quick oven. When well-risen and lightly browned on the top, it is done; roll out in warm dish, sift pulverized sugar over, and send to table.

RUM OMELET.

Put a small quantity of lard into the pan; let it simmer a few minutes and remove it; wipe the pan dry with a towel, and put in a little fresh lard in which the omelet may be fried. Care should be taken that the lard does not burn, which would spoil the color of the omelet. Break three eggs separately; put them into a bowl and whisk them thoroughly with a fork. The longer they are beaten, the lighter will the omelet be. Beat up a teaspoonful of milk with the eggs and continue to beat until the last moment before pouring into the pan, which should be over a hot fire. As soon as the omelet sets, remove the pan from the hottest part of the fire. Slip a knife under it to prevent sticking to the pan. When the centre is almost firm, slant the pan, work the omelet in shape to fold easily find neatly, and when slightly browned, hold a platter against the edge of the pan and deftly turn it out on to the hot dish. Dust a liberal quantity of powdered sugar over it, and singe the sugar into neat stripes with a hot iron rod, heated in the coals; pour a glass of warm Jamaica rum around it, and when it is placed on the table set fire to the rum. With a tablespoon dash the burning rum over the omelet, put out the fire and serve. Salt *mixed* with the eggs prevents them from rising, and when it is so used the omelet will look flabby, yet without salt it will taste insipid.

Add a little salt to it just before folding it and turning out on the dish.

SANDWICHES.

HAM SANDWICHES.

Make a dressing of half a cup of butter, one tablespoonful of mixed mustard, one of salad oil, a little red or white pepper, a pinch of salt and the yolk of an egg; rub the butter to a cream, add the other ingredients and mix thoroughly; then stir in as much chopped ham as will make it consistent and spread between thin slices of bread. Omit salad oil and substitute melted butter if preferred.

HAM SANDWICHES, PLAIN.

Trim the crusts from thin slices of bread; butter them and lay between every two some thin slices of cold boiled ham. Spread the meat with a little mustard if liked.

CHICKEN SANDWICHES.

Mince up fine any cold boiled or roasted chicken; put it into a saucepan with gravy, water or cream enough to soften it; add a good piece of butter, a pinch of pepper; work it very smooth while it is heating until it looks almost like a paste. Then spread it on a plate to cool. Spread it between slices of buttered bread.

SARDINE SANDWICHES.

Take two boxes of sardines and throw the contents into hot water, having first drained away all the oil. A few minutes will free the sardines from grease. Pour away the water and dry the fish in a cloth; then scrape away the skins and pound the sardines in a mortar till reduced to paste; add pepper, salt and some tiny pieces of lettuce, and spread on the sandwiches, which have been previously cut as above. The lettuce adds very much to the flavor of the sardines.

Or chop the sardines up fine and squeeze a few drops of lemon juice into them, and spread between buttered bread or cold biscuits.

WATER CRESS SANDWICHES.

Wash well some water cress and then dry them in a cloth, pressing out every atom of moisture as far as possible; then mix with the cress hard-boiled eggs chopped fine, and seasoned with salt and pepper. Have a stale loaf and some fresh butter, and with a sharp knife cut as many thin slices as will be required for two dozen sandwiches; then cut the cress into small pieces, removing the stems; place it between each slice of bread and butter, with a slight sprinkling of lemon juice; press down the slices hard, and cut them sharply on a board into small squares, leaving no crust.

EGG SANDWICHES.

Hard boil some very fresh eggs and when cold cut them into moderately thin slices and lay them between some bread and butter cut as thin as possible; season them with pepper, salt and nutmeg. For picnic parties, or when one is traveling, these sandwiches are far preferable to hard-boiled eggs *au naturel*.

MUSHROOM SANDWICHES.

Mince beef tongue and boiled mushrooms together, add French mustard and spread between buttered bread.

CHEESE SANDWICHES.

These are extremely nice and are very easily made. Take one hard-boiled egg, a quarter of a pound of common cheese grated, half a teaspoonful of salt, half a teaspoonful of pepper, half a teaspoonful of mustard, one tablespoonful of melted butter, and one tablespoonful of vinegar or cold water. Take the yolk of the egg and put it into a small bowl and crumble it down, put into it the butter and mix it smooth with a spoon, then add the salt, pepper, mustard and the cheese, mixing each well. Then put in the tablespoonful of vinegar, which will make it the proper thickness. If vinegar is not relished, then use cold water instead. Spread this between two biscuits or pieces of oat-cake, and you could not require a better sandwich. Some people will prefer the sandwiches less highly seasoned. In that case, season to taste.

BREAD.

Among all civilized people bread has become an article of food of the first necessity; and properly so, for it constitutes of itself a complete life sustainer, the gluten, starch and sugar which it contains representing ozotized and hydro-carbonated nutrients, and combining the sustaining powers of the animal and vegetable kingdoms in one product. As there is no one article of food that enters so largely into our daily fare as bread, so no degree of skill in preparing other articles can compensate for lack of knowledge in the art of making good, palatable and nutritious bread. A little earnest attention to the subject will enable any one to comprehend the theory, and then ordinary care in practice will make one familiar with the process.

GENERAL DIRECTIONS.

The first thing required for making wholesome bread is the utmost cleanliness; the next is the soundness and sweetness of all the ingredients used for it; and, in addition to these, there must be attention and care through the whole process.

Salt is always used in bread-making, not only on account of its flavor, which destroys the insipid raw state of the flour, but because it makes the dough rise better.

In mixing with milk, the milk should be boiled—not simply scalded, but heated to boiling over hot water—then set aside to cool before mixing. Simple heating will not prevent bread from turning sour in the rising, while boiling will act as a preventative. So the milk should be thoroughly scalded, and should be used when it is just blood warm.

Too small a proportion of yeast, or insufficient time allowed for the dough to rise, will cause the bread to be heavy.

The yeast must be good and fresh if the bread is to be digestible and nice. Stale yeast produces, instead of vinous fermentation, an acetous fermentation, which flavors the bread and makes it disagreeable. A poor, thin yeast produces an imperfect fermentation, the result being a heavy, unwholesome loaf.

If either the sponge or the dough be permitted to overwork itself—that is to say, if the mixing and kneading be neglected when it has reached the proper point for either—sour bread will probably be the consequence in warm weather, and bad bread in any. The goodness will also be endangered by placing it so near a fire as to make any part of it hot, instead of maintaining the gentle and equal degree of heat required for its due fermentation.

Heavy bread will also most likely be the result of making the dough very hard and letting it become quite cold, particularly in winter.

An almost certain way of spoiling dough is to leave it half made, and to allow it to become cold before it is finished. The other most common causes of failure are using yeast which is no longer sweet, or which has been frozen, or has had hot liquid poured over it.

As a general rule, the oven for baking bread should be rather quick and the heat so regulated as to penetrate the dough without hardening the outside. The oven door should not be opened after the bread is put in until the dough is set or has become firm, as the cool air admitted will have an unfavorable effect upon it.

The dough should rise and the bread begin to brown after about fifteen minutes, but only slightly. Bake from fifty to sixty minutes and have it brown, not black or whitey brown, but brown all over when well baked.

When the bread is baked, remove the loaves immediately from the pans and place them where the air will circulate freely around them, and thus carry off the gas which has been formed, but is no longer needed.

Never leave the bread in the pan or on a pin table to absorb the odor of the wood. If you like crusts that are crisp do not cover the loaves; but to give the soft, tender, wafer-like consistency which many prefer, wrap them while still hot in several thicknesses of bread-cloth. When cold put them in a stone jar, removing the cloth, as that absorbs the moisture and gives the bread an unpleasant taste and odor. Keep the jar well covered and carefully cleansed from crumbs and stale pieces. Scald and dry it thoroughly every two or three days. A yard and a half square of coarse table linen makes the best bread-cloth. Keep in good supply; use them for no other purpose.

Some people use scalding water in making wheat bread; in that case the flour must be scalded and allowed to cool before the yeast is added—then proceed as above. Bread made in this manner keeps moist in summer much longer than when made in the usual mode.

Home-made yeast is generally preferred to any other. Compressed yeast, as now sold in most grocery stores, makes fine light, sweet bread, and is a much quicker process, and can always be had fresh, being made fresh every day.

WHEAT BREAD.

Sift the flour into a large bread-pan or bowl; make a hole in the middle of it, and pour in the yeast in the ratio of half a teacupful of yeast to two quarts of flour; stir the yeast lightly, then pour in your "wetting," either milk or water, as you choose,—which use warm in winter and cold in summer; if you use water as "wetting," dissolve in it a bit of butter of the size of an egg,—if you use milk, no butter is necessary; stir in the "wetting" very lightly, but do not mix all the flour into it; then cover the pan with a thick blanket or towel, and set it, in winter, in a warm place to rise,—this is called "*putting the bread in sponge.*" In summer the bread should not be wet over night. In the morning add a teaspoonful of salt and mix all the flour in the pan with the sponge, kneading it well; then let stand two hours or more until it has risen quite light; then remove the dough to the molding-board and mold it for a long time, cutting it in pieces and molding them together again and again, until the dough is elastic under the pressure of your hand, using as little flour as possible; then make it into loaves, put the loaves into baking-tins. The loaves should come half way up the pan, and they should be allowed to rise until the bulk is doubled. When the loaves are ready to put into the oven, the oven should be ready to receive them. It should be hot enough to brown a teaspoonful of flour in five minutes. The heat should be greater at the bottom than at the top of the oven, and the fire so arranged as to give sufficient strength of heat through the baking without being replenished. Let them stand ten or fifteen minutes, prick them three or four times with a fork, bake in a quick oven from forty-five to sixty minutes.

If these directions are followed, you will obtain sweet, tender and wholesome bread. If by any mistake the dough becomes sour before you are ready to bake it, you can rectify it by adding a little dry super-carbonate of soda, molding the dough a long time to distribute the soda equally throughout the mass. All bread is better, if naturally sweet, without the soda; but *sour bread* you should never eat, if you desire good health.

Keep well covered in a tin box or large stone crock, which should be wiped out every day or two, and scalded and dried thoroughly in the sun once a week.

COMPRESSED YEAST BREAD.

Use for two loaves of bread three quarts of sifted flour, nearly a quart of warm water, a level tablespoonful of salt and an ounce of compressed yeast. Dissolve the yeast in a pint of lukewarm water; then stir into it enough flour to make a thick batter. Cover the bowl containing the batter or sponge with a thick folded cloth and set it in a warm place to rise; if the temperature of heat is properly attended to the sponge will be foamy and light in half an hour. Now stir into this sponge the salt dissolved in a little warm water, add the rest of the flour and sufficient warm water to make the dough stiff enough to knead; then knead it from five to ten minutes, divide it into loaves, knead again each loaf and put them into buttered baking tins; cover them with a double thick cloth and set again in a warm place to rise twice their height, then bake the same as any bread. This bread has the advantage of that made of home-made yeast as it is made inside of three hours, whereas the other requires from twelve to fourteen hours.

HOME-MADE YEAST.

Boil six large potatoes in three pints of water. Tie a handful of hops in a small muslin bag and boil with the potatoes; when thoroughly cooked drain the water on enough flour to make a thin batter; set this on the stove or range and scald it enough to cook the flour (this makes the yeast keep longer); remove it from the fire and when cool enough, add the potatoes mashed, also half a cup of sugar, half a tablespoonful of ginger, two of salt and a teacupful of yeast. Let it stand in a warm place, until it has thoroughly risen, then put it in a large mouthed jug and cork tightly; set away in a cool place. The jug should be scalded before putting in the yeast.

Two-thirds of a coffeecupful of this yeast will make four loaves.

UNRIVALED YEAST.

On one morning boil two ounces of the best hops in four quarts of water half an hour; strain it, and let the liquor cool to the consistency of new milk; then put it in an earthen bowl and add half a cupful of salt and half a cupful of brown sugar; beat up one quart of flour with some of the liquor; then mix all well together, and let it stand till the third day after; then add six medium-sized potatoes, boiled and mashed through a colander; let it stand a day, then strain and bottle and it is fit for use. It must be stirred frequently while it is making, and kept near a fire. One advantage of this yeast is its spontaneous fermentation, requiring the help of no old yeast; if care be taken to let it ferment well in the bowl, it may immediately be corked tightly. Be careful to keep it in a cool place. Before using it shake the bottle up well. It will keep in a cool place two months, and is best the latter part of the time. Use about the same quantity as of other yeast.

DRIED YEAST OR YEAST CAKES.

Make a pan of yeast the same as "Home-Made Yeast;" mix in with it corn meal that has been sifted and dried, kneading it well until it is thick enough to roll out, when it can be cut into cakes or crumble up. Spread out and dry thoroughly in the shade; keep in a dry place.

When it is convenient to get compressed yeast, it is much better and cheaper than to make your own, a saving of time and trouble. Almost all groceries keep it, delivered to them fresh made daily.

SALT-RAISING BREAD.

While getting breakfast in the morning, as soon as the tea-kettle has boiled, take a quart tin cup or an earthen quart milk pitcher, scald it, then fill one-third full of water about as warm as the finger could be held in; then to this add a teaspoonful of salt, a pinch of brown sugar and coarse flour enough to make a batter of about the right consistency for griddle-cakes. Set the cup, with the spoon in it, in a closed vessel half-filled with water moderately hot, but not scalding. Keep the temperature as nearly even as possible and add a teaspoonful of flour once or twice during the process of fermentation. The yeast ought to reach to the top of the bowl in about five hours. Sift your flour into a pan, make an opening in the centre and pour in your yeast. Have ready a pitcher of warm milk, salted, or milk and water (not too hot, or you will scald the yeast germs), and stir rapidly into a pulpy mass with a spoon. Cover this sponge closely and keep warm for an hour, then knead into loaves, adding flour to make the proper consistency. Place in warm, well-greased pans, cover closely and leave till it is light. Bake in a steady oven, and when done let all the hot steam escape. Wrap closely in damp towels and keep in closed earthen jars until it is wanted.

This, in our grandmothers' time, used to be considered the prize bread, on account of its being sweet and wholesome and required no prepared yeast to make it. Nowadays yeast-bread is made with very little trouble, as the yeast can be procured at almost any grocery.

BREAD FROM MILK YEAST.

At noon the day before baking, take half a cup of corn meal and pour over it enough sweet milk boiling hot to make it the thickness of batter-cakes. In the winter place it where it will keep warm. The next morning before breakfast pour into a pitcher a pint of boiling water; add one teaspoonful of soda and one of salt. When cool enough so that it will not scald the flour, add enough to make a stiff batter; then add the cup of meal set the day before. This will be full of little bubbles. Then place the pitcher in a kettle of warm water, cover the top with a folded towel and put it where it will keep warm, and you will be surprised to find how soon the yeast will be at the top of the pitcher. Then pour the yeast into a bread-pan; add a pint and a half of warm water, or half water and half milk, and flour enough to knead into loaves. Knead but little harder than for biscuit and bake as soon as it rises to the top of the tin. This recipe makes five large loaves. Do not allow it to get too light before baking, for it will make the bread dry and crumbling. A cup of this milk yeast is excellent to raise buckwheat cakes.

GRAHAM BREAD.

One teacupful of wheat flour, one-half teacupful of Porto Rico molasses, one-half cupful of good yeast, one teaspoonful of salt, one pint of warm water; add sufficient Graham flour to make the dough as stiff as can be stirred with a strong spoon; this is to be mixed at night; in the morning, add one teaspoonful of soda, dissolved in a little water; mix well, and pour into two medium-sized pans; they will be about half full; let it stand in a warm place until it rises to the top of the pans, then bake one hour in a pretty hot oven.

This should be covered about twenty minutes when first put into the oven with a thick brown paper, or an old tin cover; it prevents the upper crust hardening before the loaf is well-risen. If these directions are correctly followed the bread will not be heavy or sodden, as it has been tried for years and never failed.

GRAHAM BREAD. (Unfermented.)

Stir together three heaping teaspoonfuls of baking powder, three cups of Graham flour and one cup of white flour; then add a large teaspoonful of salt and half a cup of sugar. Mix all thoroughly with milk or water into as stiff a batter as can be stirred with a spoon. If water is used, a lump of butter as large as a walnut may be melted and stirred into it. Bake immediately in well-greased pans.

BOSTON BROWN BREAD.

One pint of rye flour, one quart of corn meal, one teacupful of Graham flour, all fresh; half a teacupful of molasses or brown sugar, a teaspoonful of salt, and two-thirds of a teacupful of home-made yeast. Mix into as stiff a dough as can be stirred with a spoon, using warm water for wetting. Let it rise several hours, or over night; in the morning, or when light, add a teaspoonful of soda dissolved in a spoonful of warm water; beat it well and turn it into well-greased, deep bread-pans, and let it rise again. Bake in a *moderate* oven from three to four hours.

BOSTON BROWN BREAD. (Unfermented.)

One cupful of rye flour, two cupfuls of corn meal, one cupful of white flour, half a teacupful of molasses or sugar, a teaspoonful of salt. Stir all together *thoroughly*, and wet up with sour milk; then add a level teaspoonful of soda dissolved in a tablespoonful of water. The same can be made of sweet milk by substituting baking powder for soda. The batter to be stirred as thick as can be with a spoon, and turned into well-greased pans.

VIRGINIA BROWN BREAD.

One pint of corn meal; pour over enough boiling water to thoroughly scald it; when cool add one pint of light, white bread sponge, mix well together, add one cupful of molasses, and Graham flour enough to mold; this will make two loaves; when light, bake in a moderate oven one and a half hours.

RHODE ISLAND BROWN BREAD.

Two and one-half cupfuls of corn meal, one and one-half cupfuls of rye meal, one egg, one cup of molasses, two teaspoonfuls of cream of tartar, one teaspoonful of soda, a little salt and one quart of milk. Bake in a covered dish, either earthen or iron, in a moderately hot oven three hours.

STEAMED BROWN BREAD.

One cup of white flour, two of Graham flour, two of Indian meal, one teaspoonful of soda, one cup of molasses, three and a half cups of milk, a little salt. Beat well and steam for four hours. This is for sour milk; when sweet milk is used, use baking powder in place of soda.

This is improved by setting it into the oven fifteen minutes after it is slipped from the mold. To be eaten warm with butter. Most excellent.

RYE BREAD.

To a quart of warm water stir as much wheat flour as will make a smooth batter; stir into it half a gill of home-made yeast, and set it in a warm place to rise; this is called setting a sponge; let it be mixed in some vessel which will contain twice the quantity; in the morning, put three pounds and a half of rye flour into a bowl or tray, make a hollow in the centre, pour in the sponge, add a dessertspoonful of salt, and half a small teaspoonful of soda, dissolved in a little water; make the whole into a smooth dough, with as much warm water as may be necessary; knead it well, cover it, and let it set in a warm place for three hours; then knead it again, and make it into two or three loaves; bake in a quick oven one hour, if made in two loaves, or less if the loaves are smaller.

RYE AND CORN BREAD.

One quart of rye meal or rye flour, two quarts of Indian meal, scalded (by placing in a pan and pouring over it just enough *boiling* water to merely wet it, but not enough to make it into a batter, stirring constantly with a spoon), one-half cup of molasses, two teaspoonfuls salt, one teacup yeast, make it as stiff as can be stirred with a spoon, mixing with warm water and let rise all night. In the morning add a level teaspoonful of soda dissolved in a little water; then put it in a large pan, smooth the top with the hand dipped in cold water; let it stand a short time and bake five or six hours. If put in the oven late in the day, let it remain all night.

Graham may be used instead of rye, and baked as above.

This is similar to the "Rye and Injun" of our grandmothers' days, but that was placed in a kettle, allowed to rise, then placed in a covered iron pan upon the hearth before the fire, with coals heaped upon the lid, to bake all night.

FRENCH BREAD.

Beat together one pint of milk, four tablespoonfuls of melted butter, or half butter and half lard, half a cupful of yeast, one teaspoonful of salt and two eggs. Stir into this two quarts of flour. When this dough is risen, make into two large rolls and bake as any bread. Cut across the top diagonal gashes just before putting into the oven.

TWIST BREAD.

Let the bread be made as directed for wheat bread, then take three pieces as large as a pint bowl each; strew a little flour over the paste-board or table, roll each piece under your hands to twelve inches length, making it smaller in circumference at the ends than in the middle; having rolled the three in this way, take a baking-tin, lay one part on it, joint one end of each of the other two to it, and braid them together the length of the rolls and join the ends by pressing them together; dip a brush in milk and pass it over the top of the loaf; after ten minutes or so, set it in a quick oven and bake for nearly an hour.

NEW ENGLAND CORN CAKE.

One quart of milk, one pint of corn meal, one teacupful of wheat flour, a teaspoonful of salt, two tablespoonfuls of melted butter. Scald the milk and gradually pour it on the meal; when cool add the butter and salt, also a half cup of yeast. Do this at night; in the morning beat thoroughly and add two well-beaten eggs, and a half teaspoonful of soda, dissolved in a spoonful of water. Pour the mixture into buttered deep earthen plates, let it stand fifteen minutes to rise again, then bake from twenty to thirty minutes.

GERMAN BREAD.

One pint of milk well boiled, one teacupful of sugar, two tablespoonfuls of nice lard or butter, two-thirds of a teacupful of baker's yeast. Make a rising with the milk and yeast; when light, mix in the sugar and shortening, with flour enough to make as soft a dough as can be handled. Flour the paste-board well, roll out about one-half inch thick; put this quantity into two large pans; make about a dozen indentures with the finger on the top; put a small piece of butter in each, and sift over the whole one tablespoonful of sugar mixed with one teaspoonful of cinnamon. Let this stand for a second rising; when perfectly light, bake in a quick oven fifteen or twenty minutes.

CORN BREAD.

Two cups of sifted meal, half a cup of flour, two cups of sour milk, two well-beaten eggs, half a cup of molasses or sugar, a teaspoonful of salt, two tablespoonfuls of melted butter. Mix the meal and flour smoothly and gradually with the milk, then the butter, molasses and salt, then the beaten eggs, and lastly dissolve a level teaspoonful of baking soda in a little milk and beat thoroughly altogether. Bake nearly an hour in well-buttered tins, not very shallow. This recipe can be made with sweet milk by using baking powder in place of soda.

VIRGINIA CORN BREAD.

Three cups of white corn meal, one cup of flour, one tablespoonful of sugar, one teaspoonful of salt, two heaping teaspoonfuls of baking powder, one tablespoonful of lard, three cups of milk and three eggs. Sift together the flour, corn meal, sugar, salt and baking powder; rub in the lard cold, add the eggs well beaten and then the milk. Mix into a moderately stiff batter; pour it into well-greased, shallow baking pans (pie-tins are suitable). Bake from thirty to forty minutes.

BOSTON CORN BREAD.

One cup of sweet milk, two of sour milk, two-thirds of a cup of molasses, one of wheat flour, four of corn meal and one teaspoonful of soda; steam for three hours, and brown a few minutes in the oven. The same made of sweet milk and baking powder is equally as good.

INDIAN LOAF CAKE.

Mix a teacupful of powdered white sugar with a quart of rich milk, and cut up in the milk two ounces of butter, adding a saltspoonful of salt. Put this mixture into a covered pan or skillet, and set it on the fire till it is scalding hot. Then take it off, and scald with it as much yellow Indian meal (previously sifted) as will make it of the consistency of thick boiled mush. Beat the whole very hard for a quarter of an hour, and then set it away to cool.

While it is cooling, beat three eggs very light, and stir them gradually into the mixture when it is about as warm as new milk. Add a teacupful of good strong yeast and beat the whole another quarter of an hour, for much of the goodness of this cake depends on its being long and well beaten. Then have ready a tin mold or earthen pan with a pipe in the centre (to diffuse the heat through the middle of the cake). The pan must be very well-buttered as Indian meal is apt to stick. Put in the mixture, cover it and set it in a warm place to rise. It should be light in about four hours. Then bake it two hours in a moderate oven. When done, turn it out with the broad surface downwards and send it to table hot and whole. Cut it into slices and eat it with butter.

This will be found an excellent cake. If wanted for breakfast, mix it and set it to rise the night before. If properly made, standing all night will not injure it. Like all Indian cakes (of which this is one of the best), it should be eaten warm.

JOHNNIE CAKE.

Sift one quart of Indian meal into a pan; make a hole in the middle and pour in a pint of warm water, adding one teaspoonful of salt; with a spoon mix the meal and water gradually into a soft dough; stir it very briskly for a quarter of an hour or more, till it becomes light and spongy; then spread the dough smoothly and evenly on a straight, flat board (a piece of the head of a flour-barrel will serve for this purpose); place the board nearly upright before an open fire and put an iron against the back to support it; bake it well; when done, cut it in squares; send it hot to table, split and buttered.

SPIDER CORN-CAKE.

Beat two eggs and one-fourth cup sugar together. Then add one cup sweet milk and one cup of sour milk in which you have dissolved one teaspoonful soda. Add a teaspoonful of salt. Then mix one and two-thirds cups of granulated corn meal and one-third cup flour with this. Put a spider or skillet on the range and when it is hot melt in two tablespoonfuls of butter. Turn the spider so that the butter can run up on the sides of the pan. Pour in the corn-cake mixture and add one more cup of sweet milk, but do not stir afterwards. Put this in the oven and bake from twenty to thirty-five minutes. When done, there should be a streak of custard through it.

SOUTHERN CORN MEAL PONE OR CORN DODGERS.

Mix with cold water into a soft dough one quart of southern corn meal, sifted, a teaspoonful of salt, a tablespoonful of butter or lard melted. Mold into oval cakes with the hands and bake in a very hot oven, in well-greased pans. To be eaten hot. The crust should be brown.

RAISED POTATO-CAKE.

Potato-cakes, to be served with roast lamb or with game, are made of equal quantities of mashed potatoes and of flour, say one quart of each, two tablespoonfuls of butter, a little salt and milk enough to make a batter as for griddle-cakes; to this allow half a teacupful of fresh yeast; let it rise till it is light and bubbles of air form; then dissolve half a teaspoonful of soda in a spoonful of warm water and add to the batter; bake in muffin tins. These are good also with fricasseed chicken; take them from the tins and drop in the gravy just before sending to the table.

BISCUITS, ROLLS, MUFFINS, ETC.

GENERAL SUGGESTIONS.

In making batter-cakes, the ingredients should be put together over night to rise, and the eggs and butter added in the morning; the butter melted and eggs well beaten. If the batter appears sour in the least, dissolve a little soda and stir into it; this should be done early enough to rise some time before baking.

Water can be used in place of milk in all raised dough, and the dough should be thoroughly light before making into loaves or biscuits; then when molding them use as little flour as possible; the kneading to be done when first made from the sponge, and should be done well and for some length of time, as this makes the pores fine, the bread cut smooth and tender. Care should be taken not to get the dough too stiff.

Where any recipe calls for baking powder, and you do not have it, you can use cream of tartar and soda, in the proportion of one level teaspoonful of soda to two of cream of tartar.

When the recipe calls for sweet milk or cream, and you do not have it, you may use in place of it sour milk or cream, and, in that case, baking powder or cream of tartar *must not* be used, but baking-soda, using a *level* teaspoonful to a quart of sour milk; the milk is always best when just turned, so that it is solid, and not sour enough to whey or to be watery.

When making biscuits or bread with baking powder or soda and cream of tartar, the oven should be prepared first; the dough handled quickly and put into the oven immediately, as soon as it becomes the proper lightness, to ensure good success. If the oven is *too slow*, the article baked will be heavy and hard.

As in beating cake, never *stir* ingredients into batter, but beat them in, by beating down from the bottom, and up, and over again. This laps the air into the batter which produces little air-cells and causes the dough to puff and swell as it comes in contact with the heat while cooking.

TO RENEW STALE ROLLS.

To freshen stale biscuits or rolls, put them into a steamer for ten minutes, then dry them off in a hot oven; or dip each roll for an instant in cold water and heat them crisp in the oven.

WARM BREAD FOR BREAKFAST..

Dough after it has become once sufficiently raised and perfectly light, cannot afterwards be injured by setting aside in any cold place where it cannot *freeze*; therefore, biscuits, rolls, etc., can be made late the day before wanted for breakfast. Prepare them ready for baking by molding them out late in the evening; lay them a little apart on buttered tins; cover the tins with a cloth, then fold around that a newspaper, so as to exclude the air, as that has a tendency to cause the crust to be hard and thick when baked. The best place in summer is to place them in the ice-box, then all you have to do in the morning (an hour before breakfast time, and while the oven is heating) is to bring them from the ice-box, take off the cloth and warm it, and place it over them again; then set the tins in a warm place near the fire. This will give them time to rise and bake when needed. If these directions are followed rightly, you will find it makes no difference with their lightness and goodness, and you can always be sure of warm raised biscuits for breakfast in one hour's time.

Stale rolls may be made light and flakey by dipping for a moment in cold water, and placing immediately in a very hot oven to be made crisp and hot.

SODA BISCUIT.

One quart of sifted flour, one teaspoonful of soda, two teaspoonfuls of cream of tartar, one teaspoonful of salt; mix thoroughly, and rub in two tablespoonfuls of butter and wet with one pint of sweet milk. Bake in a quick oven.

BAKING POWDER BISCUIT.

Two pints of flour, butter the size of an egg, three heaping teaspoonfuls of baking powder and one teaspoonful of salt; make a soft dough of sweet milk or water, knead as little as possible, cut out with the usual biscuit-cutter and bake in rather a quick oven.

SOUR MILK BISCUIT.

Rub into a quart of sifted flour a piece of butter the size of an egg, one teaspoonful of salt; stir into this a pint of sour milk, dissolve one teaspoonful of soda and stir into the milk just as you add it to the flour; knead it up quickly, roll it out nearly half an inch thick and cut out with a biscuit-cutter; bake immediately in a quick oven.

Very nice biscuit may be made with sour cream without the butter by the same process.

RAISED BISCUIT.

Sift two quarts of flour in a mixing-pan, make a hole in the middle of the flour, pour into this one pint of warm water or new milk, one teaspoonful of salt, half a cup of melted lard or butter, stir in a little flour, then add half a cupful of yeast, after which stir in as much flour as you can conveniently with your hand, let it rise over night; in the morning add nearly a teaspoonful of soda, and more flour as is needed to make a rather soft dough; then mold fifteen to twenty minutes, the longer the better; let it rise until light again, roll this out about half an inch thick and cut out with a biscuit-cutter, or make it into little balls with your hands; cover and set in a warm place to rise. When light, bake a light brown in a moderate oven. Rub a little warm butter or sweet lard on the sides of the biscuits when you place them on the tins, to prevent their sticking together when baked.

LIGHT BISCUIT. No. 1.

Take a piece of bread dough that will make about as many biscuits as you wish; lay it out rather flat in a bowl; break into it two eggs, half a cup of sugar, half a cup of butter; mix this thoroughly with enough flour to keep it from sticking to the hands and board. Knead it well for about fifteen or twenty minutes, make into small biscuits, place in a greased pan, and let them rise until about even with the top of the pan. Bake in a quick oven for about half an hour.

These can be made in the form of rolls, which some prefer.

LIGHT BISCUIT. No. 2.

When you bake take a pint of sponge, one tablespoonful of melted butter, one tablespoonful of sugar, the white of one egg beaten to a foam. Let rise until light, mold into biscuits, and when light bake.

GRAHAM BISCUITS, WITH YEAST.

Take one pint of water or milk, one large tablespoonful of butter, two tablespoonfuls of sugar, a half cup of yeast and a pinch of salt; take enough wheat flour to use up the water, making it the consistency of batter-cakes; add the rest of the ingredients and as much Graham flour as can be stirred in with a spoon; set it away till morning, in the morning grease a pan, flour your hands, take a lump of dough the size of an egg, roll it lightly between the palms of your hands, let them rise twenty minutes, and bake in a tolerably hot oven.

EGG BISCUIT.

Sift together a quart of dry flour and three heaping teaspoonfuls of baking powder. Rub into this thoroughly a piece of butter the size of an egg; add two well-beaten eggs, a tablespoonful of sugar, a teaspoonful of salt. Mix all together quickly into a soft dough, with one cup of milk, or more if needed. Roll out nearly half of an inch thick. Cut into biscuits, and bake immediately in a quick oven from fifteen to twenty minutes.

PARKER HOUSE ROLLS.

One pint of milk, boiled and cooled, a piece of butter the size of an egg, one-half cupful of fresh yeast, one tablespoonful of sugar, one pinch of salt, and two quarts of sifted flour.

Melt the butter in the warm milk, then add the sugar, salt and flour, and let it rise over night. Mix rather soft. In the morning, add to this half of a teaspoonful of soda dissolved in a spoonful of water. Mix in enough flour to make the same stiffness as any biscuit dough; roll out not more than a quarter of an inch thick. Cut with a large round cutter; spread soft butter over the tops and fold one-half over the other by doubling it. Place them apart a little so that there will be room to rise. Cover and place them near the fire for fifteen or twenty minutes before baking. Bake in rather a quick oven.

PARKER HOUSE ROLLS. (Unfermented.)

These rolls are made with baking powder, and are much sooner made, although the preceding recipe is the old original one from the "Parker House." Stir into a quart of sifted flour three large teaspoonfuls of baking powder, a tablespoonful of cold butter, a teaspoonful of salt and one of sugar, and a well-beaten egg; rub all well into the flour, pour in a pint of cold milk, mix up quickly into a smooth dough, roll it out less than half an inch thick, cut with a large biscuit-cutter, spread soft butter over the top of each; fold one-half over the other by doubling it, lay them a little apart on greased tins. Set them immediately in a pretty hot oven. Rub over the tops with sweet milk before putting in the oven, to give them a glaze.

FRENCH ROLLS.

Three cups of sweet milk, one cup of butter and lard, mixed in equal proportions, one-half cup of good yeast, or half a cake of compressed yeast, and a teaspoonful of salt. Add flour enough to make a stiff dough. Let it rise over night; in the morning, add two well-beaten eggs; knead thoroughly and let it rise again. With the hands, make it into balls as large as an egg; then roll between the hands to make *long rolls* (about three inches). Place close together in even rows on well-buttered pans. Cover and let them rise again, then bake in a quick oven to a delicate brown.

BEATEN BISCUIT.

Two quarts of sifted flour, a teaspoonful of salt, a tablespoonful of sweet lard, one egg; make up with half a pint of milk, or if milk is not to be had, plain water will answer; beat well until the dough blisters and cracks; pull off a two-inch square of the dough; roll it into a ball with the hand; flatten, stick with a fork, and bake in a quick oven.

It is not beating hard that makes the biscuit nice, but the regularity of the motion. Beating hard, the old cooks say, *kills* the dough.

POTATO BISCUIT.

Boil six good-sized potatoes with their jackets on; take them out with a skimmer, drain and squeeze with a towel to ensure being dry; then remove the skin, mash them perfectly free from lumps, add a tablespoonful of butter, one egg and a pint of sweet milk. When cool, beat in half a cup of yeast. Put in just enough flour to make a stiff dough. When this rises, make into small cakes. Let them rise the same as biscuit and bake a delicate brown.

This dough is very fine dropped into meat soups for pot-pie.

VINEGAR BISCUITS.

Take two quarts of flour, one large tablespoonful of lard or butter, one tablespoonful and a half of vinegar and one teaspoonful of soda; put the soda in the vinegar and stir it well; stir in the flour; beat two eggs very light and add to it; make a dough with warm water stiff enough to roll out, and cut with a biscuit-cutter one inch thick and bake in a *quick* oven.

GRAFTON MILK BISCUITS.

Boil and mash two white potatoes; add two teaspoonfuls of brown sugar; pour boiling water over these, enough to soften them. When tepid, add one small teacupful of yeast; when light, warm three ounces of butter in one pint of milk, a little salt, a third of a teaspoonful of soda and flour enough to make stiff sponge; when risen, work it on the board, put it back in the tray to rise again; when risen, roll into cakes and let them stand half an hour. Bake in a *quick* oven. These biscuits are fine.

SALLY LUNN.

Warm one-half cupful of butter in a pint of milk; add a teaspoonful of salt, a tablespoonful of sugar, and seven cupfuls of *sifted* flour; beat thoroughly and when the mixture is blood warm, add four beaten eggs and last of all, half a cup of good lively yeast. Beat hard until the batter breaks in blisters. Set it to rise over night. In the morning, dissolve half a teaspoonful of soda, stir it into the batter and turn it into a well-buttered, shallow dish to rise again about fifteen or twenty minutes. Bake about fifteen to twenty minutes.

The cake should be torn apart, not cut; cutting with a knife makes warm bread heavy. Bake a light brown. This cake is frequently seen on Southern tables.

SALLY LUNN. (Unfermented.)

Rub a piece of butter as large as an egg into a quart of flour; add a tumbler of milk, two eggs, three tablespoonfuls of sugar, three tablespoonfuls of baking powder and a teaspoonful of salt. Scatter the baking powder, salt and sugar into the flour; add the eggs, the butter, melted, the milk. Stir all together and bake in well-greased round pans. Eat warm with butter.

LONDON HOT-CROSS BUNS.

Three cups of milk, one cup of yeast, or one cake of compressed yeast dissolved in a cup of tepid water, and flour enough to make a thick batter; set this as a sponge over night. In the morning add half a cup of melted butter, one cup of sugar, half a nutmeg grated, one saltspoonful of salt, half a teaspoonful of soda, and flour enough to roll out like biscuit. Knead well and set to rise for five hours. Roll the dough half an inch thick; cut in round cakes and lay in rows in a buttered baking-pan, and let the cakes stand half an hour, or until light; then put them in the oven, having first made a deep cross on each with a knife. Bake a light brown and brush over with white of egg beaten stiff with powdered sugar.

RUSKS, WITH YEAST.

In one large coffeecup of warm milk dissolve half a cake of compressed yeast, or three tablespoonfuls of home-made yeast; to this add three well-beaten eggs, a small cup of sugar and a teaspoonful of salt; beat these together. Use flour enough to make a smooth, light dough, let it stand until very light, then knead it in the form of biscuits; place them on buttered tins and let them rise until they are almost up to the edge of the tins; pierce the top of each one and bake in a quick oven. Glaze the top of each with sugar and milk, or the white of an egg, before baking. Some add dried currants, well-washed and dried in the oven.

RUSKS.

Two cups of raised dough, one of sugar, half a cup of butter, two well-beaten eggs, flour enough to make a stiff dough; set to rise, and when light mold into high biscuit and let rise again; rub damp sugar and cinnamon over the top and place in the oven. Bake about twenty minutes.

RUSKS. (Unfermented.)

Three cups of flour sifted, three teaspoonfuls of baking powder, one teaspoonful of salt, three tablespoonfuls of sugar, two tablespoonfuls of butter, three eggs, half a nutmeg grated and a teaspoonful of ground cinnamon, two small cups of milk; sift together salt, flour, sugar and baking powder; rub in the butter cold; add the milk, beaten eggs and spices; mix into a soft dough, break off pieces about as large as an egg, roll them under the hands into round balls, rub the tops with sugar and water mixed, and then sprinkle dry sugar over them. Bake immediately.

SCOTCH SCONES.

Thoroughly mix, while dry, one quart of sifted flour, loosely measured, with two heaping teaspoonfuls of baking powder; then rub into it a tablespoonful of cold butter and a teaspoonful of salt. Be sure that the butter is well worked in. Add sweet milk enough to make a *very* soft paste. Roll out the paste about a quarter of an inch thick, using plenty of flour on the paste-board and rolling pin. Cut it into triangular pieces, each side about four inches long. Flour the sides and bottom of a biscuit tin, and place the pieces on it. Bake immediately in a quick oven from twenty to thirty minutes. When half done, brush over with sweet milk. Some cooks prefer to bake them on a floured griddle, and cut them a round shape the size of a saucer, then scarred across to form four quarters.

CRACKNELS.

Two cups of rich milk, four tablespoonfuls of butter and a gill of yeast, a teaspoonful of salt; mix warm, add flour enough to make a light dough. When light, roll thin and cut in long pieces three inches wide, prick well with a fork and bake in a slow oven. They are to be mixed rather hard and rolled very thin, like soda crackers.

RAISED MUFFINS. No. 1.

Make a batter of one pint of sweet milk, one teaspoonful of sugar, one of salt, a tablespoonful of butter or sweet lard and a half cup of yeast; add flour enough to make it moderately thick; keep it in a warm, *not hot*, place until it is quite light, then stir in one or two well-beaten eggs, and half a teaspoonful of soda, dissolved in a little warm water. Let the batter stand twenty-five or thirty minutes longer to rise a little, turn into well-greased muffin-rings or gem-pans, and bake in a quick oven.

To be served hot and torn open, instead of cut with a knife.

RAISED MUFFINS. No. 2.

Three pints of flour, three eggs, a piece of butter the size of an egg, two heaping teaspoonfuls of white sugar, one-half cake of compressed yeast and a quart of milk; warm the milk with the butter in it; cool a little, stir in the sugar and add a little salt; stir this gradually into the flour, then add the eggs well beaten; dissolve the yeast in half a cup of lukewarm water and add to the other ingredients; if the muffins are wanted for luncheon, mix them about eight o'clock in the morning; if for breakfast, set them at ten o'clock at night; when ready for baking, stir in half a teaspoonful of soda dissolved in a teaspoonful of hot water; butter the muffin-rings or gem-irons and bake in a quick oven.

EGG MUFFINS. (Fine.)

One quart of flour, sifted twice; three eggs, the whites and yolks beaten separately, three teacups of sweet milk, a teaspoonful of salt, a tablespoonful of sugar, a large tablespoonful of lard or butter and two heaping teaspoonfuls of baking powder. Sift together flour, sugar, salt and baking powder; rub in the lard cold, add the beaten eggs and milk; mix quickly into a smooth batter, a little firmer than for griddle-cakes. Grease well some muffin-pans and fill them two-thirds full. Bake in a hot oven fifteen or twenty minutes. These made of cream, omitting the butter, are excellent.

PLAIN MUFFINS.

One egg well beaten, a tablespoonful of butter and a tablespoonful of sugar, with a teaspoonful of salt, all beaten until very light. One cup of milk, three of sifted flour and three teaspoonfuls of baking powder. One-half Graham and one-half rye meal may be used instead of wheat flour, or two cups of corn meal and one of flour.

Drop on well-greased patty-pans and bake twenty minutes in a rather quick oven, or bake on a griddle in muffin-rings.

MUFFINS WITHOUT EGGS.

One quart of buttermilk, a teaspoonful of soda dissolved in the milk, a little salt, and flour enough to make a stiff batter. Drop in hot gem-pans and bake in a quick oven. Two or three tablespoonfuls of sour cream will make them a little richer.

TENNESSEE MUFFINS.

One pint of corn meal, one pint of flour, one tablespoonful of sugar, one teaspoonful of salt, three of baking powder, one tablespoonful of lard or butter, two eggs and a pint of milk. Sift together corn meal, flour, sugar, salt and powder; rub in lard or butter cold, and eggs beaten and milk; mix into batter of consistency of cup-cake; muffin-rings to be cold and well greased, then fill two-thirds full. Bake in hot oven fifteen minutes.

CORN MEAL MUFFINS. (Without Eggs.)

One cup of flour, one cup of corn meal, two tablespoonfuls of sugar, water to make a thick batter, or sour milk is better; mix at night; in the morning add two tablespoonfuls of melted butter and one teaspoonful of soda; bake in cake rounds.

HOMINY MUFFINS.

Two cups of boiled hominy; beat it smooth, stir in three cups of sour milk, half a cup of melted butter, two teaspoonfuls of salt, two tablespoonfuls of sugar; add three eggs well beaten, one teaspoonful of soda dissolved in hot water, two cups of flour. Bake quickly.

Rice muffins may be made in the same manner.

GRAHAM GEMS. No. 1.

Two cupfuls of Graham flour, one cupful of wheat flour, two teaspoonfuls of baking powder, a tablespoonful of sugar, one of salt and one well-beaten egg.

Mix with sweet milk to make a thin batter; beat it well. Bake in gem-irons; have the irons well greased; fill two-thirds full and bake in a hot oven. Will bake in from fifteen to twenty minutes.

GRAHAM GEMS. No. 2.

Three cups of sour milk, one teaspoonful of soda, one of salt, one tablespoonful of brown sugar, one of melted lard or butter, one or two beaten eggs; to the egg add the milk, then the sugar and salt, then the Graham flour (with the soda mixed in), together with the lard or butter; make a stiff batter, so that it will *drop*, not pour, from the spoon. Have the gem-pans very hot, fill and bake fifteen minutes in a hot oven.

The same can be made of sweet milk, using three teaspoonfuls of baking powder instead of soda, and if you use sweet milk, put in no shortening. Excellent.

Muffins of all kinds should only be cut just around the edge, then pulled open with the fingers.

PLAIN GRAHAM GEMS.

Two cupfuls of the best Graham meal, two of water, fresh and cold, or milk and water, and a little salt. Stir briskly for a minute or two. Have the gem-pan, hot and well greased, on the top of the stove while pouring in the batter. Then place in a very hot oven and bake forty minutes. It is best to check the heat a little when they are nearly done. As the best prepared gems may be spoiled if the heat is not sufficient, care and judgment must be used in order to secure this most healthful as well, as delicious bread.

WAFFLES.

Take a quart of flour and wet it with a little sweet milk that has been boiled and cooled, then stir in enough of the milk to form a thick batter. Add a tablespoonful of melted butter, a teaspoonful of salt, and yeast to raise it. When light add two well-beaten eggs, heat your waffle-iron, grease it well and fill it with the batter. Two or three minutes will suffice to bake on one side; then turn the iron over, and when brown on both sides the cake is done. Serve immediately.

CONTINENTAL HOTEL WAFFLES.

Put into one quart of sifted flour three teaspoonfuls of baking powder, one teaspoonful of salt, one of sugar, all thoroughly stirred and sifted together; add a tablespoonful of melted butter, six well-beaten eggs and a pint of sweet milk; cook in waffle-irons heated and well greased. Serve hot.

NEWPORT WAFFLES.

Make one pint of Indian meal into mush in the usual way. While hot, put in a small lump of butter and a dessertspoonful of salt. Set the mush aside to cool. Meanwhile, beat separately till very light the whites and yolks of four eggs. Add the eggs to the mush, and cream in gradually one quart of wheaten flour. Add half a pint of buttermilk, or sour cream, in which has been dissolved half a teaspoonful of carbonate of soda. Lastly, bring to the consistency of thin batter by the addition of sweet milk. Waffle-irons should be put on to heat an hour in advance, that they may be in the proper condition for baking as soon as the batter is ready. Have a brisk fire, butter the irons thoroughly, but with nicety, and bake quickly. Fill the irons only half full of batter, that the waffles may have room to rise.

CREAM WAFFLES.

One pint of sour cream, two eggs, one pint of flour, one tablespoonful of corn meal, one teaspoonful of soda, half a teaspoonful of salt. Beat the eggs separately, mix the cream with the beaten yolks, stir in the flour, corn meal and salt; add the soda dissolved in a little sweet milk, and, lastly, the whites beaten to a stiff froth.

RICE WAFFLES. No. 1.

One quart of flour, half a teaspoonful of salt, one teaspoonful of sugar, two teaspoonfuls of baking powder, one large tablespoonful of butter, two eggs, one and a half pints of milk, one cupful of hot boiled rice. Sift the flour, salt, sugar and baking powder well together; rub the butter into the flour; beat the eggs well, separately, and add the stiff whites last of all.

RICE WAFFLES. No. 2.

Rub through a sieve one pint of boiled rice, add it to a tablespoonful of dry flour, two-thirds of a teaspoonful of salt, two teaspoonfuls of baking powder. Beat separately the yolks and whites of three eggs; add to the yolks a cup and a half of milk, work it into the flour, then add an ounce of melted butter; beat the whites of eggs thoroughly; mix the whole together. Heat the waffle-iron and grease it evenly; pour the batter into the half of the iron over the range until nearly two-thirds full, cover, allow to cook a moment, then turn and brown slightly on the other side.

GERMAN RICE WAFFLES.

Boil a half pound of rice in milk until it becomes thoroughly soft Then remove it from the fire, stirring it constantly, and adding, a little at a time, one quart of sifted flour, five beaten eggs, two spoonfuls of yeast, a half pound of melted butter, a little salt and a teacupful of warm milk. Set the batter in a warm place, and, when risen, bake in the ordinary way.

BERRY TEA-CAKES.

Nice little tea-cakes to be baked in muffin-rings are made of one cup of sugar, two eggs, one and a half cups of milk, one heaping teaspoonful of baking powder, a piece of butter the size of an egg and flour sufficient to make a stiff batter. In this batter stir a pint bowl of fruit—any fresh are nice—or canned berries with the juice poured off. Serve while warm and they are a dainty addition to the tea-table. Eaten with butter.

RYE DROP-CAKES.

One pint of warm milk, with half a teaspoonful of soda dissolved in it, a little salt, four eggs well beaten, and rye flour enough to make a thin batter; bake in small cups, buttered, and in a hot oven, or in small cakes upon a hot griddle.

WHEAT DROP-CAKES.

One pint of cream, six eggs well beaten, a little salt, and wheat flour enough to make a thin batter; bake in little cups buttered and in a hot oven fifteen minutes.

POP-OVERS.

Two cups of flour, two cups of sweet milk, two eggs, one teaspoonful of butter, one teaspoonful of salt, bake in cups in a quick oven fifteen minutes. Serve hot with a sweet sauce.

FLANNEL CAKES. (With Yeast.)

Heat a pint of sweet milk and into it put two heaping tablespoonfuls of butter, let it melt, then add a pint of cold milk and the well-beaten yolks of four eggs—placing the whites in a cool place; also, a teaspoonful of salt, four tablespoonfuls of home-made yeast and sufficient flour to make a stiff batter; set it in a warm place to rise; let it stand three hours or over night; before baking add the beaten whites; bake like any other griddle-cakes. Be sure to make the batter stiff enough, for flour must not be added after it has risen, unless it is allowed to rise again. These, half corn meal and half wheat, are very nice.

FEATHER GRIDDLE-CAKES. (With Yeast.)

Make a batter, at night, of a pint of water or milk, a teaspoonful of salt, and half a teacupful of yeast; in the morning, add to it one teacupful of thick, sour milk, two eggs well beaten, a level tablespoonful of melted butter, a level teaspoonful of soda and flour enough to make the consistency of pancake batter; let stand twenty minutes, then bake.

This is a convenient way, when making sponge for bread over night, using some of the sponge.

WHEAT GRIDDLE-CAKES.

Three cups of flour, one teaspoonful of salt, three teaspoonfuls of baking powder sifted together; beat three eggs and add to three cupfuls of sweet milk, also a tablespoonful of melted butter; mix all into a smooth batter, as thick as will run in a stream from the lips of a pitcher. Bake on a well-greased, hot griddle, a nice light brown. Very good.

SOUR MILK GRIDDLE-CAKES.

Make a batter of a quart of sour milk and as much sifted flour as is needed to thicken so that it will run from the dish; add two beaten eggs, a teaspoonful of salt, a tablespoonful of melted butter, and a level teaspoonful of soda dissolved in a little milk or cold water, added last; then bake on a hot griddle, well greased, brown on both sides.

CORN MEAL GRIDDLE-CAKES. (With Yeast.)

Stir into one quart of boiling milk three cups of corn meal; after it cools add one cup of white flour, a teaspoonful of salt and three tablespoonfuls of home-made yeast. Mix this over night. In the morning add one tablespoonful of melted butter or lard, two beaten eggs and a teaspoonful of soda dissolved in a little water.

This batter should stand a few minutes, after adding the butter and soda, that it should have time to rise a little; in the meantime the griddle could be heating. Take a small stick like a good-sized skewer, wind a bit of cloth around the end of it, fasten it by winding a piece of thread around that and tying it firm. Melt together a tablespoonful of butter and lard. Grease the griddle with this. Between each batch of cakes, wipe the griddle off with a clean paper or cloth and grease afresh. Put the cakes on by spoonfuls, or pour them carefully from a pitcher, trying to get them as near the same size as possible. As soon as they begin to bubble all over turn them, and cook on the other side till they stop puffing. The second lot always cooks better than the first, as the griddle becomes evenly heated.

CORN MEAL GRIDDLE-CAKES.

Scald two cups of sifted meal, mix with a cup of wheat flour and a teaspoonful of salt. Add three well-beaten eggs; thin the whole with sour milk enough to make it the right consistency. Beat the whole till very light and add a teaspoonful of baking soda dissolved in a little water. If you use sweet milk, use two large teaspoonfuls of baking powder instead of soda.

GRIDDLE-CAKES. (Very Good.)

One quart of Graham flour, half a pint of Indian meal, one gill of yeast, a teaspoonful of salt; mix the flour and meal, pour on enough warm water to make batter rather thicker than that for buckwheat cakes, add the yeast, and when light bake on griddle not too hot.

GRAHAM GRIDDLE-CAKES.

Mix together dry two cups of Graham flour, one cup wheat flour, two heaping teaspoonfuls of baking powder and one teaspoonful of salt. Then add three eggs well beaten, one tablespoonful of lard or butter melted and three cups of sweet milk. Cook immediately on a hot griddle.

BREAD GRIDDLE-CAKES.

One quart of milk, boiling hot; two cups fine bread crumbs, three eggs, one tablespoonful melted butter, one-half teaspoonful salt, one-half teaspoonful soda dissolved in warm water; break the bread into the boiling milk, and let stand for ten minutes in a covered bowl, then beat to a smooth paste; add the yolks of the eggs well whipped, the butter, salt, soda, and finally the whites of the eggs previously whipped stiff, and add half of a cupful of flour. These can also be made of sour milk, soaking the bread in it over night and using a little more soda.

RICE GRIDDLE-CAKES.

Two cupfuls of cold boiled rice, one pint of flour, one teaspoonful sugar, one-half teaspoonful salt, one and one-half teaspoonfuls baking powder, one egg, a little more than half a pint of milk. Sift together flour, sugar, salt and powder; add rice free from lumps, diluted with beaten egg and milk; mix into smooth batter. Have griddle well heated, make cakes large, bake nicely brown, and serve with maple syrup.

POTATO GRIDDLE-CAKES.

Twelve large potatoes, three heaping tablespoonfuls of flour, one teaspoonful of baking powder, one-half teaspoonful salt, one or two eggs, two teacupfuls of boiling milk. The potatoes are peeled, washed and grated into a little cold water (which keeps them white), then strain off water and pour on boiling milk, stir in eggs, salt and flour, mixed with the baking powder; if agreeable, flavor with a little fine chopped onion; bake like any other pancakes, allowing a little more lard or butter. Serve with stewed or preserved fruit, especially with huckleberries.

GREEN CORN GRIDDLE-CAKES.

One pint of milk, two cups grated green corn, a little salt, two eggs, a teaspoonful of baking powder, flour sufficient to make a batter to fry on the griddle. Butter them hot and serve.

HUCKLEBERRY GRIDDLE-CAKES.

Made the same as above, leaving out one cup of milk, adding one tablespoonful of sugar and a pint of huckleberries rolled in flour. Blackberries or raspberries can be used in the same manner.

FRENCH GRIDDLE-CAKES.

Beat together until smooth six eggs and a pint sifted flour; melt one ounce of butter and add to the batter, with one ounce of sugar and a cup of milk; beat until smooth; put a tablespoonful at a time into a frying pan slightly greased, spreading the batter evenly over the surface by tipping the pan about; fry to a light brown; spread with jelly, roll up, dust with powdered sugar and serve hot.

RAISED BUCKWHEAT CAKES.

Take a small crock or large earthen pitcher, put into it a quart of warm water or half water and milk, one heaping teaspoonful of salt; then stir in as much buckwheat flour as will thicken it to rather a stiff batter; lastly, add half a cup of yeast; make it smooth, cover it up warm to rise over night; in the morning add a small, level teaspoonful of soda dissolved in a little warm water; this will remove any sour taste, if any, and increase the lightness.

Not a few object to eating buckwheat, as its tendency is to thicken the blood, and also to produce constipation; this can be remedied by making the batter one-third corn meal and two-thirds buckwheat, which makes the cakes equally as good. Many prefer them in this way.

BUCKWHEAT CAKES WITHOUT YEAST.

Two cups of buckwheat flour, one of wheat flour, a little salt, three teaspoonfuls baking powder; mix thoroughly and add about equal parts of milk and water until the batter is of the right consistency then stir until free from lumps. If they do not brown well, add a little molasses.

BUCKWHEAT CAKES.

Half a pint of buckwheat flour, a quarter of a pint of corn meal, a quarter of a pint of wheat flour, a little salt, two eggs beaten very light, one quart of new milk (made a little warm and mixed with the eggs before the flour is put in), one tablespoonful of butter or sweet lard, two large tablespoonfuls of yeast. Set it to rise at night for the morning. If in the least sour, stir in before baking just enough soda to correct the acidity. A very nice, but more expensive, recipe.

SWEDISH GRIDDLE-CAKES.

One pint of white flour, sifted; six eggs, whites and yolks beaten separately to the utmost; one saltspoonful of salt; one saltspoonful of soda dissolved in vinegar; milk to make a thin batter.

Beat the yolks light, add the salt, soda, two cupfuls of milk, then the flour and beaten whites alternately; thin with more milk if necessary.

CORN MEAL FRITTERS.

One pint of sour milk, one teaspoonful of salt, three eggs, one tablespoonful of molasses or sugar, one handful of flour, and corn meal enough to make a stiff batter; lastly, stir in a small teaspoonful of soda, dissolved in a little warm water.

This recipe is very nice made of rye flour.

CREAM FRITTERS.

One cup of cream, five eggs—the whites only, two full cups prepared flour, one saltspoonful of nutmeg, a pinch of salt.

Stir the whites into the cream in turn with the flour, put in nutmeg and salt, beat all up hard for two minutes. The batter should be rather thick. Fry in plenty of hot, sweet lard, a spoonful of batter for each fritter. Drain, and serve upon a hot, clean napkin. Eat with jelly sauce. Pull, not cut, them open. Very nice.

CURRANT FRITTERS.

Two cupfuls dry, fine bread crumbs, two tablespoonfuls of prepared flour, two cups of milk, one-half pound currants, washed and well dried, five eggs whipped very light, one-half cup powdered sugar, one tablespoonful butter, one-half teaspoonful mixed cinnamon and nutmeg. Boil the milk and pour over the bread. Mix and put in the butter. Let it get cold. Beat in next the yolks and sugar, the seasoning, flour and stiff whites; finally, the currants dredged whitely with flour. The batter should be thick. Drop in great spoonfuls into the hot lard and fry. Drain them and send hot to table. Eat with a mixture of wine and powdered sugar.

WHEAT FRITTERS.

Three eggs, one and a half cups of milk, three teaspoonfuls baking powder, salt, and flour enough to make quite stiff, thicker than batter cakes. Drop into hot lard and fry like doughnuts.

A Good Sauce for the Above.—One cup of sugar, two tablespoonfuls of butter, one teaspoonful of flour beaten together; half a cup boiling water; flavor with extract lemon and boil until clear. Or serve with maple syrup.

APPLE FRITTERS.

Make a batter in the proportion of one cup sweet milk to two cups flour, a heaping teaspoonful of baking powder, two eggs beaten separately, one tablespoonful of sugar and a saltspoon of salt; heat the milk a little more than milk-warm, add it slowly to the beaten yolks and sugar; then add flour and whites of the eggs; stir all together and throw in thin slices of good sour apples, dipping the batter up over them; drop into boiling hot lard in large spoonfuls with pieces of apple in each, and fry to a light brown. Serve with maple syrup, or a nice syrup made with clarified sugar.

Bananas, peaches, sliced oranges and other fruits can be used in the same batter.

PINEAPPLE FRITTERS.

Make a batter as for apple fritters; then pare one large pineapple, cut it in slices a quarter of an inch thick, cut the slices in halves, dip them into the batter and fry them, and serve them as above.

PEACH FRITTERS.

Peel the peaches, split each in two and take out the stones; dust a little powdered sugar over them; dip each piece in the batter and fry in hot fat. A sauce to be served with them may be made as follows: Put an ounce of butter in a saucepan and whisk it to a cream; add four ounces of sugar gradually. Beat the yolks of two eggs; add to them a dash of nutmeg and a gill each of cold water and rum; stir this into the luke-warm batter and allow it to heat gradually. Stir constantly until of a smooth, creamy consistency, and serve. The batter is made as follows: Beat the yolks of three eggs; add to them a gill of milk, or half of a cupful, a saltspoonful of salt, four ounces of flour; mix. If old flour is used a little more milk may be found necessary.

GOLDEN-BALL FRITTERS.

Put into a stewpan a pint of water, a piece of butter as large as an egg and a tablespoonful of sugar. When it boils stir into it one pint of sifted flour, stirring briskly and thoroughly. Remove from the fire, and when nearly cooled beat into it six eggs, each one beaten separately and added one at a time, beating the batter between each. Drop the stiff dough into boiling lard by teaspoonfuls. Eat with syrup, or melted sugar and butter flavored.

Stirring the boiling lard around and around, so that it whirls when you drop in the fritters, causes them to assume a round shape like balls.

CANNELONS, OR FRIED PUFFS.

Half a pound of puff paste, apricot or any kind of preserve that may be preferred, hot lard.

Cannelons, which are made of puff paste rolled very thin, with jam enclosed, and cut out in long, narrow rolls or puffs, make a very pretty and elegant dish. Make some good puff paste, roll it out very thin, and cut it into pieces of an equal size, about two inches wide and eight inches long; place upon each piece a spoonful of jam, wet the edges with the white of egg and fold the paste over *twice*; slightly press the edges together, that the jam may not escape in the frying, and when all are prepared, fry them in boiling lard until of a nice brown, letting them remain by the side of the fire after they are colored, that the paste may be thoroughly done. Drain them before the fire, dish on a d'oyley, sprinkle over them sifted sugar and serve. These cannelons are very delicious made with fresh instead of preserved fruit, such as strawberries, raspberries or currants; they should be laid in the paste, plenty of pounded sugar sprinkled over and folded and fried in the same manner as stated above.

GERMAN FRITTERS.

Take slices of stale bread cut in rounds or stale cake; fry them in hot lard, like crullers, to a *light* brown. Dip each slice when fried in boiling milk, to remove the grease; drain quickly, dust with powdered sugar or spread with preserves. Pile on a hot plate and serve. Sweet wine sauce poured over them is very nice.

HOMINY FRITTERS.

Take one pint of hot boiled hominy, two eggs, half a teaspoonful of salt and a tablespoonful of flour; thin it a little with cold milk; when cold add a teaspoonful of baking powder, mix thoroughly, drop tablespoonfuls of it into hot fat and fry to a delicate brown.

PARSNIP FRITTERS.

Take three or four good-sized parsnips. Boil them until tender. Mash and season with a little butter, a pinch of salt and a slight sprinkling of pepper. Have ready a plate with some sifted flour on it. Drop a tablespoonful of the parsnip in the flour and roll it about until well coated and formed into a ball. When you have a sufficient number ready, drop them into boiling drippings or lard, as you would a fritter; fry a delicate brown and serve hot. Do not put them in a covered dish, for that would steam them and deprive them of their crispness, which is one of their great charms.

These are also very good fried in a frying pan with a small quantity of lard and butter mixed, turning them over so as to fry both sides brown.

GREEN CORN FRITTERS.

One pint of grated, young and tender, green corn, three eggs, two tablespoonfuls of milk or cream, one tablespoonful of melted butter, if milk is used, a teaspoonful of salt. Beat the eggs well, add the corn by degrees, also the milk and butter; thicken with just enough flour to hold them together, adding a teaspoonful of baking powder to the flour. Have ready a kettle of hot lard, drop the corn from the spoon into the fat and fry a light brown. They are also nice fried in butter and lard mixed, the same as fried eggs.

CREAM SHORT-CAKE.

Sift one quart of fine white flour, rub into it three tablespoonfuls of cold butter, a teaspoonful of salt, a tablespoonful of white sugar. Add a beaten egg to a cup of sour cream, turn it into the other ingredients, dissolve a teaspoonful of soda in a spoonful of water, mix all together, handling as little as possible; roll lightly into two round sheets, place on pie-tins and bake from twenty to twenty-five minutes in a quick oven.

This crust is delicious for fruit short-cake.

STRAWBERRY SHORT-CAKE.

Make a rule of baking powder biscuit, with the exception of a little more shortening; divide the dough in half; lay one-half on the molding board (half the dough makes one short-cake), divide this half again, and roll each piece large enough to cover a biscuit-tin, or a large sized pie-tin; spread soft butter over the lower one and place the other on top of that; proceed with the other lump of dough the same, by cutting it in halves, and putting on another tin. Set them in the oven; when sufficiently baked take them out, separate each one by running a large knife through where the cold soft butter was spread. Then butter plentifully each crust, lay the bottom of each on earthen platters or dining-plates; cover thickly with a quart of strawberries that have been previously prepared with sugar, lay the top crusts on the fruit. If there is any juice left pour it around the cake. This makes a delicious short-cake.

Peaches, raspberries, blackberries and huckleberries can be substituted for strawberries. Always send to the table with a pitcher of sweet cream.

ORANGE SHORT-CAKE.

Peel two large oranges, chop them fine, remove the seeds, add half a peeled lemon and one cup of sugar. Spread between the layers of short-cake while it is hot.

ICING THE CAKES.

LEMON SHORT-CAKE.

Make a rich biscuit dough, same as above recipe. While baking, take a cup and a quarter of water, a cup and a half of sugar, and two lemons, peel, juice and pulp, throwing away the tough part of the rind; boil this for some little time; then stir in three crackers rolled fine; split the short-cakes while hot, spread with butter, then with the mixture. To be eaten warm.

HUCKLEBERRY SHORT-CAKE.

Two cupfuls of sugar, half a cupful of butter, one pint of sweet milk, one tablespoonful of salt, two heaping teaspoonfuls of baking powder sifted into a quart of flour, or enough to form a thick batter; add a quart of the huckleberries; to be baked in a dripper; cut into squares for the table and served hot with butter. Blackberries may be used the same.

FRIED DINNER-ROLLS.

When making light raised bread, save out a piece of dough nearly the size of a small loaf. Roll it out on the board, spread a tablespoonful of melted butter over it. Dissolve a quarter of a teaspoonful of soda in a tablespoonful of water and pour that also over it; work it all well into the dough, roll it out into a sheet not quite half an inch thick. Cut it in strips three inches long and one inch wide. Lay them on buttered tins, cover with a cloth and set away in a cool place until an hour before dinner time; then set them by the fire where they will become light. While they are rising, add to a frying-pan a tablespoonful of cold butter and one of lard; When it boils clear and is *hot*, lay as many of the rolls in as will fry nicely. As soon as they brown on one side turn them over and brown the other; then turn them on the edges and brown the sides. Add fresh grease as is needed. Eat them warm in place of bread. Nice with warm meat dinner.

NEWPORT BREAKFAST-CAKES.

Take one quart of dough from the bread at an early hour in the morning; break three eggs, separating yolks and whites, both to be whipped to a light froth; mix them into the dough and gradually add two tablespoonfuls of melted butter, one of sugar, one teaspoonful of soda, and enough warm milk with it until it is a batter the consistency of buckwheat cakes; beat it well and let it rise until breakfast time. Have the griddle hot and nicely greased, pour on the batter in small round cakes and bake a light brown, the same as any griddle cake.

PUFF BALLS.

To a piece of butter as large as an egg stirred until soft; add three well-beaten eggs, a pinch of salt and half a teacupful of sour cream. Stir well together, then add enough flour to make a very thick batter. Drop a spoonful of this into boiling water. Cook until the puffs rise to the surface. Dish them hot with melted butter turned over them. Nice accompaniment to a meat dinner as a side-dish—similar to plain macaroni.

BREAKFAST PUFFS.

Two cups of sour milk, one teaspoonful of soda, one teaspoonful of salt, one egg and flour enough to roll out like biscuit dough. Cut into narrow strips an inch wide and three inches long, fry brown in hot lard like doughnuts. Serve hot; excellent with coffee. Or fry in a spider with an ounce each of lard and butter, turning and browning all four of the sides.

ENGLISH CRUMPETS.

One quart of warm milk, half a cup of yeast, one teaspoonful of salt, flour enough to make a stiff batter; when light, add half a cupful of melted butter, a teaspoonful of soda dissolved in a little water and a very little more flour; let it stand twenty minutes or until light. Grease some muffin-rings, place them on a hot griddle and fill them half full of the batter; when done on one side turn and bake the other side. Butter them while hot; pile one on another and serve immediately.

PLAIN CRUMPETS.

Mix together thoroughly while dry one quart of sifted flour, loosely measured, two heaping teaspoonfuls baking powder and a little salt; then add two tablespoonfuls of melted butter and sweet milk enough to make a thin dough. Bake quickly in muffin-rings or patty-pans.

PREPARED BREAD CRUMBS.

Take pieces of stale bread, break them in small bits, put them on a baking pan and place them in a moderate oven, watching closely that they do not scorch; then take them while hot and crisp and roll them, crushing them. Sift them, using the fine crumbs for breading cutlets, fish, croquettes, etc. The coarse ones may be used for puddings, pancakes, etc.

CRACKERS.

Sift into a pint of flour a heaping teaspoonful of baking powder, four tablespoonfuls of melted butter, half a teaspoonful salt and the white of an egg beaten and one cup of milk; mix it with more flour, enough to make a very stiff dough, as stiff as can be rolled out; pounded and kneaded a long time. Roll very thin like pie crust and cut out either round or square. Bake a light brown.

Stale crackers are made crisp and better by placing them in the oven a few moments before they are needed for the table.

FRENCH CRACKERS.

Six eggs, twelve tablespoonfuls of sweet milk, six tablespoonfuls of butter, half a teaspoonful of soda; mold with flour, pounding and working half an hour; roll it thin. Bake with rather quick fire.

CORN MEAL MUSH OR HASTY PUDDING.

Put two quarts of water into a clean dinner-pot or stewpan, cover it and let it become boiling hot over the fire; then add a tablespoonful of salt, take off the light scum from the top, have sweet, fresh yellow or white corn meal; take a handful of the meal with the left hand and a pudding-stick in the right, then with the stick, stir the water around and by degrees let fall the meal; when one handful is exhausted, refill it; continue to stir and add meal until it is as thick as you can stir easily, or until the stick will stand in it; stir it awhile longer; let the fire be gentle; when it is sufficiently cooked, which will be in half an hour, it will bubble or puff up; turn it into a deep basin. This is eaten cold or hot, with milk or with butter and syrup or sugar, or with meat and gravy, the same as potatoes or rice.

FRIED MUSH.

Make it like the above recipe, turn it into bread tins and when cold slice it, dip each piece in flour and fry it in lard and butter mixed in the frying pan, turning to brown well both sides. Must be served hot.

GRAHAM MUSH.

Sift Graham meal slowly into boiling salted water, stirring briskly until thick as can be stirred with one hand; serve with milk or cream and sugar, or butter and syrup. It will be improved by removing from the kettle to a pan, as soon as thoroughly mixed, and steaming three or four hours. It may also be eaten cold, or sliced and fried, like corn meal mush.

OATMEAL.

Soak one cup of oatmeal in a quart of water over night, boil half an hour in the morning, salted to taste. It is better to cook it in a dish set into a dish of boiling water.

RICE CROQUETTES.

Boil for thirty minutes one cup of well-washed rice in a pint of milk; whip into the hot rice the following ingredients: Two ounces of butter, two ounces of sugar, some salt, and when slightly cool add the yolks of two eggs well beaten; if too stiff pour in a little more milk; when cold, roll into small balls and dip in beaten eggs, roll in fine cracker or bread crumbs, and fry same as doughnuts. Or they may be fried in the frying pan, with a tablespoonful each of butter and lard mixed, turning and frying both sides brown. Serve very hot.

HOMINY.

This form of cereal is very little known and consequently little appreciated in most Northern households. "Big hominy" and "little hominy," as they are called in the South, are staple dishes there and generally take the place of oatmeal, which is apt to be too heating for the climate. The former is called "samp" here. It must be boiled for at least eight hours to be properly cooked, and may then be kept on hand for two or three days and warmed over, made into croquettes or balls, or fried in cakes. The fine hominy takes two or three hours for proper cooking, and should be cooked in a dish set into another of boiling water, and kept steadily boiling until thoroughly soft.

HOMINY CROQUETTES.

To a cupful of cold boiled hominy, add a teaspoonful of melted butter, and stir it well, adding by degrees a cupful of milk, till all is made into a soft, light paste; add a teaspoonful of white sugar, a pinch of salt, and one well-beaten egg. Roll it into oval balls with floured hands, dipped in beaten egg, then rolled in cracker crumbs, and fry in hot lard.

The hominy is best boiled the day or morning before using.

BOILED RICE.

Take half or quarter of a pound of the best quality of rice; wash it in a strainer, and put it in a saucepan, with a quart of clean water and a pinch of salt; let it boil slowly till the water is all evaporated—see that it does not burn—then pour in a teacupful of new milk; stir carefully from the bottom of the saucepan, so that the upper grain may go under, but do not smash it; close the lid on your saucepan carefully down, and set it on a cooler part of the fire, where it will not boil; as soon as it has absorbed the added milk, serve it up with fresh new milk, adding fruit and sugar for those who like them.

Another nice way to cook rice is to take one teacupful of rice and one quart of milk, place in a steamer, and steam from two to three hours; when nearly done, stir in a piece of butter as large as the yolk of an egg, and a pinch of salt. You can use sugar if you like. The difference in the time of cooking depends on your rice—the older the rice, the longer it takes to cook.

SAMP, OR HULLED CORN.

An old-fashioned way of preparing hulled corn was to put a peck of old, dry, ripe corn into a pot filled with water, and with it a bag of hardwood ashes, say a quart. After soaking a while it was boiled until the skins or hulls came off easily. The corn was then washed in cold water to get rid of the taste of potash, and then boiled until the kernels were soft. Another way was to take the lye from the leaches where potash was made, dilute it, and boil the corn in this until the skins or hulls came off. It makes a delicious dish, eaten with milk or cream.

CRACKED WHEAT.

Soak the wheat over night in cold water, about a quart of water to a cup of wheat; cook it as directed for oatmeal; should be thoroughly done. Eaten with sugar and cream.

OAT FLAKES.

This healthful oat preparation may be procured from the leading grocers and is prepared as follows: Put into a double saucepan or porcelain-lined pan a quart of boiling water, add a saltspoonful of salt, and when it is boiling add, or rather stir in gradually, three ounces of flakes. Keep stirring to prevent burning. Let it boil from fifteen to twenty minutes and serve with cream and sugar.

Ordinarily oatmeal requires two hours' steady cooking to make it palatable and digestible. Wheaten grits and hominy one hour, but a half hour longer cooking will not injure them and makes them easier of digestion. Never be afraid of cooking cereals or preparations from cereals too long, no matter what the directions on the package may be.

STEAMED OATMEAL.

To one teacupful oatmeal add a quart of cold water, a teaspoonful of salt; put in a steamer over a kettle of cold water, gradually heat and steam an hour and a half after it begins to cook.

HOMINY.

Hominy is a preparation of Indian corn, broken or ground, either large or small, and is an excellent breakfast dish in winter or summer. Wash the hominy thoroughly in on 3 or two waters, then cover it with twice its depth of cold water and let it come to a boil slowly. If it be the large hominy, simmer six hours; if the small hominy, simmer two hours. When the water evaporates add hot water; when done it may be eaten with cream, or allowed to become cold and warmed up in the frying pan, using a little butter to prevent burning.

TOAST.

Toast should be made of stale bread, or at least of bread that has been baked a day. Cut smoothly in slices, not more than half an inch thick; if the crust is baked very hard, trim the edges and brown very evenly, but if it happens to burn, that should be scraped off. Toast that is to be served with anything turned over it, should have the slices first dipped quickly in a dish of hot water turned from the boiling tea-kettle, with a little salt thrown in. Cold biscuits cut in halves, and the under crust sliced off, then browned evenly on both sides, make equally as good toast. The following preparations of toast are almost all of them very nice dishes, served with a family breakfast.

MILK TOAST.

Put over the fire a quart of milk, put into it a tablespoonful of cold butter, stir a heaping teaspoonful of flour into half a gill of milk; as soon as the milk on the fire boils, stir in the flour, add a teaspoonful of salt; let all boil up once, remove from the fire, and dip in this slices of toasted bread. When all are used up, pour what is left of the scalded milk over the toast. Cover and send to the table hot.

CREAM TOAST.

Heat a pint of milk to boiling and add a piece of butter the size of an egg; stir a tablespoonful of flour smoothly into a cup of rich cream, and add some of the boiling milk to this; heat it gradually and prevent the flour from lumping; then stir into the boiling milk and let it cook a few moments; salt to taste. After taking from the fire stir in a beaten egg; strain the mixture on to toast lightly buttered.

AMERICAN TOAST.

To one egg thoroughly beaten, put one cup of sweet milk and a little salt. Slice light bread and dip into the mixture, allowing each slice to absorb some of the milk; then brown on a hot buttered griddle or thick-bottomed frying pan; spread with butter and serve hot.

NUNS' TOAST.

Cut four or five hard-boiled eggs into slices. Put a piece of butter half the size of an egg into a saucepan and when it begins to bubble add a finely chopped onion. Let the onion cook a little without taking color, then stir in a teaspoonful of flour. Add a cupful of milk and stir until it becomes smooth; then put in the slices of eggs and let them get hot. Pour over neatly trimmed slices of hot buttered toast. The sauce must be seasoned to taste with pepper and salt.

CHEESE TOAST. No. 1.

Toast thin slices of bread an even, crisp brown. Place on a warm plate, allowing one small slice to each person, and pour on enough melted cheese to cover them. Rich new cheese is best. Serve while warm. Many prefer a little prepared mustard spread over the toast before putting on the cheese.

CHEESE TOAST. No. 2.

Put half an ounce of butter in a frying pan; when hot add gradually four ounces of mild American cheese. Whisk it thoroughly until melted. Beat together half a pint of cream and two eggs; whisk into the cheese, add a little salt, pour over the crisp toast, and serve.

The two above recipes are usually called "Welsh Rarebit."

OYSTER TOAST.

Select the large ones, used for frying, and first dip them in beaten egg, then in either cracker or bread crumbs and cook upon a fine wire gridiron, over a quick fire. Toast should be made ready in advance, and a rich cream sauce poured over the whole. After pouring on the sauce, finely cut celery strewn over the top adds to their delicacy.

Or wash oysters in the shell and put them on hot coals, or upon the top of a hot stove, or bake them in a hot oven; open the shells with an oyster-knife, taking care to lose none of the liquor. Dip the toast into hot, salted water quickly and turn out the oyster and liquor over the toast; season with salt and pepper and a teaspoonful of melted butter over each.

Oysters steamed in the shell are equally as good.

MUSHROOMS ON TOAST.

Peel a quart of mushrooms and cut off a little of the root end. Melt an ounce of butter in the frying pan and fry in it half a pound of raw minced steak; add two saltspoonfuls of salt, a pinch of cayenne and a gill of hot water; fry until the juices are extracted from the meat; tilt the pan and squeeze the meat with the back of the spoon until there is nothing left but dry meat, then remove it; add the mushrooms to the liquid and if there is not enough of it, add more butter; toss them about a moment and pour out on hot toast.

Some add a little sherry to the dish before removing from the fire.

TOMATO TOAST.

Pare and stew a quart of ripe tomatoes until smooth. Season with salt, pepper and a tablespoonful of butter. When done, add one cup sweet cream and a little flour. Let it scald, but not boil; remove at once. Pour over slices of dipped toast, well buttered.

EGGS ON TOAST.

Various preparations of eggs can be served on toast, first dipping slices of well-toasted bread quickly in hot salted water, then turning over them scrambled, poached or creamed eggs, all found in the recipes among EGGS.

BAKED EGGS ON TOAST.

Toast six slices of stale bread, dip them in hot salted water and butter them lightly. After arranging them on a platter or deep plate, break enough eggs to cover them, breaking one at a time and slip over the toast so that they do not break; sprinkle over them salt and pepper and turn over all some kind of thickened gravy—either chicken or lamb, cream or a cream sauce made the same as "White Sauce;" turn this over the toast and eggs and bake in a hot oven until the eggs are set, or about five minutes. Serve at once.

HAM TOAST.

Take a quarter of a pound of either boiled or fried ham, chop it fine, mix it with the yolks of two eggs, well beaten, a tablespoonful of butter, and enough cream or rich milk to make it soft, a dash of pepper. Stir it over the fire until it thickens. Dip the toast for an instant in hot salted water; spread over some melted butter, then turn over the ham mixture. Serve hot.

REED BIRDS ON TOAST.

Remove the feathers and legs of a dozen reed birds, split them down the back, remove the entrails, and place them on a double broiler; brush a little melted butter over them and broil the inner side thoroughly first; then lightly broil the other side. Melt one quarter of a pound of butter, season it nicely with salt and pepper, dip the birds in it, and arrange them nicely on slices of toast.

MINCED FOWLS ON TOAST.

Remove from the bones all the meat of either cold roast or boiled fowls. Clean it from the skin, and keep covered from the air until ready for use. Boil the bones and skin with three-fourths of a pint of water until reduced quite half. Strain the gravy and let it cool. Next, having skimmed off the fat, put it into a clean saucepan with half a cup of cream, three tablespoonfuls of butter, well mixed with a tablespoonful of flour. Keep these stirred until they boil. Then put in the fowl finely minced, with three hard-boiled eggs, chopped, and sufficient salt and pepper to season. Shake the mince over the fire until just ready to serve. Dish it over hot toast and serve.

HASHED BEEF ON TOAST.

Chop a quantity of cold roast beef rather fine and season it well with pepper and salt. For each pint of meat add a level tablespoonful of flour. Stir well and add a small teacupful of soup-stock or water. Put the mixture into a small stewpan and, after covering it, simmer for twenty minutes. Meanwhile, toast half a dozen slices of bread nicely and at the end of the twenty minutes spread the meat upon them. Serve at once on a hot dish. In case water be used instead of soup-stock, add a tablespoonful of butter just before spreading the beef upon the toast. Any kind of cold meat may be prepared in a similar manner.

VEAL HASH ON TOAST.

Take a teacupful of boiling water in a saucepan, stir in an even teaspoonful of flour, wet in a tablespoonful of cold water, and let it boil five minutes; add one-half teaspoonful of black pepper, as much salt and two tablespoonfuls of butter, and let it keep hot, but not boil. Chop the veal fine and mix with it half as much stale bread crumbs. Put it in a pan and pour the gravy over it, then let it simmer ten minutes. Serve this on buttered toast.

CODFISH ON TOAST. (Cuban Style.)

Take a teacupful of freshened codfish picked up fine. Fry a sliced onion in a tablespoonful of butter; when it has turned a light brown, put in the fish with water enough to cover it; add half a can of tomatoes, or half a dozen of fresh ones. Cook all nearly an hour, seasoning with a little pepper. Serve on slices of dipped toast, hot. Very fine.

Plain creamed codfish is very nice turned over dipped toast.

HALIBUT ON TOAST.

Put into boiling salted water one pound of fresh halibut; cook slowly for fifteen minutes, or until done; remove from the water and chop it fine; then add half a cup of melted butter and eight eggs well beaten. Season with salt and pepper.

Place over the fire a thick-bottomed frying pan containing a tablespoonful of cold butter; when it begins to melt, tip the pan so as to grease the sides; then put in the fish and eggs and stir one way until the eggs are cooked, but not *too* hard. Turn over toast dipped in hot salted water.

CHICKEN HASH WITH RICE TOAST.

Boil a cup of rice the night before; put it into a square, narrow bread-pan, set it in the ice-box. Next morning cut it in half inch slices, rub over each slice a little warm butter and toast them on a broiler to a delicate brown. Arrange the toast on a warm platter and turn over the whole a chicken hash made from the remains of cold fowl, the meat picked from the bones, chopped fine, put into the frying pan with butter and a little water to moisten it, adding pepper and salt. Heat hot all through. Serve immediately.

APPLE TOAST.

Cut six apples into quarters, take the core out, peel and cut them in slices; put in the saucepan an ounce of butter, then throw over the apples about two ounces of white powdered sugar and two tablespoonfuls of water; put the saucepan on the fire, let it stew quickly, toss them up, or stir with a spoon; a few minutes will do them. When tender cut two or three slices of bread half an inch thick; put in a frying pan two ounces of butter, put on the fire; when the butter is melted put in your bread, which fry of a nice yellowish color; when nice and crisp take them out, place them on a dish, a little white sugar over, the apples about an inch thick. Serve hot.

CAKES.

SUGGESTIONS IN REGARD TO CAKE-MAKING.

Use none but the best materials, and all the ingredients should be properly prepared before commencing to mix any of them. Eggs beat up much lighter and sooner by being placed in a cold place sometime before using them; a small pinch of soda sometimes has the same effect. Flour should always be sifted before using it. Cream of tartar or baking powder should be thoroughly mixed with the flour; butter be placed where it will become moderately soft, but *not* melted in the least, or the cake will be sodden and heavy. Sugar should be rolled and sifted; spices ground or pounded; raisins or any ether fruit looked over and prepared; currants, especially, should be nicely washed, picked, dried in a cloth and then carefully examined, that no pieces of grit or stone may be left amongst them. They should then be laid on a dish before the fire to become thoroughly dry; as, if added damp to the other ingredients, cakes will be liable to be heavy.

Eggs should be well beaten, the whites and yolks separately, the yolks to a thick cream, the whites until they are a stiff froth. Always stir the butter and sugar to a cream, then add the beaten yolks, then the milk, the flavoring, then the beaten whites, and, lastly, the flour. If fruit is to be used, measure and dredge with a little sifted flour, stir in gradually and thoroughly.

Pour all in well-buttered cake-pans. While the cake is baking care should be taken that no cold air enters the oven, only when necessary to see that the cake is baking properly; the oven should be an even, moderate heat, not too cold or too hot; much depends on this for success. Cake is often spoiled by being looked at too often when first put into the oven. The heat should be tested before the cake is put in, which can be done by throwing on the floor of the oven a tablespoonful of new flour. If the flour takes fire, or assumes a dark brown color, the temperature is too high and the oven must be allowed to cool; if the flour remains white after the lapse of a few seconds, the temperature is too low. When the oven is of the proper temperature the flour will slightly brown and look slightly scorched.

Another good way to test the heat, is to drop a few spoonfuls of the cake batter on a small piece of buttered letter paper, and place it in the oven during the finishing of the cake, so that the piece will be baked before putting in the whole cake; if the little drop of cake batter bakes evenly without burning around the edge, it will be safe to put the whole cake in the oven. Then, again, if the oven seems too hot, fold a thick brown paper double, and lay on the bottom of the oven; then after the cake has risen, put a thick brown paper over the top, or butter well a thick white paper and lay carefully over the top.

If, after the cake is put in, it seems to bake too fast, put a brown paper loosely over the top of the pan, care being taken that it does not touch the cake, and do not open the door for five minutes at least; the cake should then be quickly examined, and the door shut carefully, or the rush of cold air will cause it to fall. Setting a *small dish* of hot water in the oven, will also prevent the cake from scorching.

To ascertain when the cake is done, run a broom straw into the middle of it; if it comes out clean and smooth, the cake will do to take out.

Where the recipe calls for baking powder, and you have none, you can use cream of tartar and soda in proportion to one level teaspoonful of soda, two heaping teaspoonfuls of cream of tartar.

When sour milk is called for in the recipe, use only soda. Cakes made with molasses burn much more easily than those made with sugar. Never stir cake after the butter and sugar is creamed, but beat it down from the bottom, up and over; this laps air into the cake batter, and produces little air cells, which cause the dough to puff and swell when it comes in contact with the heat while cooking.

When making most cakes, especially sponge cake, the flour should be added by degrees, stirred very slowly and lightly, for if stirred hard and fast it will make it porous and tough.

Cakes should be kept in tight tin cake-cans, or earthen jars, in a cool, dry place.

Cookies, jumbles, ginger-snaps, etc., require a quick oven; if they become moist or soft by keeping, put again into the oven a few minutes.

To remove a cake from a tin after it is baked, so that it will not crack, break or fall, first butter the tin well all around the sides and bottom; then cut a piece of letter paper to exactly fit the tin, butter that on both sides, placing it smoothly on the bottom and sides of the tin. When the cake is baked, let it remain in the tin until it is *cold*; then set it in the oven a minute, or just long enough to warm the tin through. Remove it from the oven; turn it upside down on your hand, tap the edge of the tin on the table and it will slip out with ease, leaving it whole.

If a cake-pan is too shallow for holding the quantity of cake to be baked, for fear of its being so light as to rise above the pan, that can be remedied by thoroughly greasing a piece of thick glazed letter paper with soft butter. Place or fit it around the sides of the buttered tin, allowing it to reach an inch or more above the top. If the oven heat is moderate the butter will preserve the paper from burning.

FROSTING OR ICING.

In the first place, the eggs should be cold, and the platter on which they are to be beaten also cold. Allow, for the white of one egg, one small teacupful of powdered sugar. Break the eggs and throw a small handful of the sugar on them as soon as you begin beating; keep adding it at intervals until it is all used up. The eggs must *not* be beaten until the sugar has been added in this way, which gives a smooth, tender frosting, and one that will dry much sooner than the old way.

Spread with a broad knife evenly over the cake, and if it seems too thin, beat in a little more sugar. Cover the cake with two coats, the second after the first has become dry, or nearly so. If the icing gets too dry or stiff before the last coat is needed, it can be thinned sufficiently with a little water, enough to make it work smoothly.

A little lemon juice, or half a teaspoonful of tartaric acid, added to the frosting while being beaten, makes it white and more frothy.

The flavors mostly used are lemon, vanilla, almond, rose, chocolate and orange. If you wish to ornament with figures or flowers, make up rather more icing, keep about one-third out until that on the cake is dried; then, with a clean glass syringe, apply it in such forms as you desire and dry as before; what you keep out to ornament with may be tinted pink with cochineal, blue with indigo, yellow with saffron or the grated rind of an orange strained through a cloth, green with spinach juice and brown with chocolate, purple with cochineal and indigo. Strawberry, or currant and cranberry juices color a delicate pink.

Set the cake in a cool oven with the door open to dry, or in a draught in an open window.

ALMOND FROSTING.

The whites of three eggs, beaten up with three cups of fine, white sugar. Blanch a pound of sweet almonds, pound them in a mortar with a little sugar, until a fine paste, then add the whites of eggs, sugar and vanilla extract. Pound a few minutes to thoroughly mix. Cover the cake with a very thick coating of this, set in a cool oven to dry, afterwards cover with a plain icing.

CHOCOLATE FROSTING.

The whites of four eggs, three cups of powdered sugar and nearly a cup of grated chocolate. Beat the whites a very little, they must not become white, stir in the chocolate, then put in the sugar gradually, beating to mix it well.

PLAIN CHOCOLATE ICING.

Put into a shallow pan four tablespoonfuls of scraped chocolate, and place it where it will melt gradually, but not scorch; when melted, stir in three tablespoonfuls of milk or cream and one of water; mix all well together, and add one scant teacupful of sugar; boil about five minutes, and while hot, and when the cakes are nearly cold, spread some evenly over the surface of one of the cakes; put a second one on top, alternating the mixture and cakes; then cover top and sides, and set in a warm oven to harden. All who have tried recipe after recipe, vainly hoping to find one where the chocolate sticks to the cake and not to the fingers, will appreciate the above. In making those most palatable of cakes, "Chocolate Eclairs," the recipe just given will be found very satisfactory.

TUTTI FRUTTI ICING.

Mix with boiled icing one ounce each of chopped citron, candied cherries, seedless raisins, candied pineapple and blanched almonds.

SUGAR ICING.

To one pound of extra refined sugar add one ounce of fine white starch; pound finely together and then sift them through gauze; then beat the whites of three eggs to a froth. The secret of success is to beat the eggs long enough, and always one way; add the powdered sugar by degrees, or it will spoil the froth of the eggs. When all the sugar is stirred in continue the whipping for half an hour longer, adding more sugar if the ice is too thin. Take a little of the icing and lay it aside for ornamenting afterward. When the cake comes out of the oven, spread the sugar icing smoothly over it with a knife and dry it at once in a cool oven. For ornamenting the cake the icing may be tinged any color preferred. For pink, use a few drops of cochineal; for yellow, a pinch of saffron dissolved; for green, the juice of some chopped spinach. Whichever is chosen, let the coloring be first mixed with a little colorless spirit and then stirred into the white icing until the tint is deep enough. To ornament the cake with it, make a cone of stiff writing paper and squeeze the colored icing through it, so as to form leaves, beading or letters, as the case may be. It requires nicety and care to do it with success.

BOILED FROSTING.

To one pound of finest pulverized sugar add three wine-glassfuls of clear water. Let it stand until it dissolves; then boil it until it is perfectly clear and threads from the spoon. Beat well the whites of four eggs. Pour the sugar into the dish with the eggs, but do not mix them until the syrup is luke-warm; then beat all well together for one-half hour.

Season to your taste with vanilla, rose-water, or lemon juice. The first coating may be put on the cake as soon as it is well mixed. Rub the cake with a little flour before you apply the icing. While the first coat is drying continue to beat the remainder; you will not have to wait long if the cake is set in a warm place near the fire. This is said to be a most excellent recipe for icing.

FROSTING WITHOUT EGGS.

An excellent frosting may be made without eggs or gelatine, which will keep longer and cut more easily, causing no breakage or crumbling and withal is very economical.

Take one cup of granulated sugar; dampen it with one-fourth of a cup of milk, or five tablespoonfuls; place it on the fire in a suitable dish and stir it until it boils; then let it boil for five minutes without stirring; remove it from the fire and set the dish in another of cold water; add flavoring. While it is cooling, stir or beat it constantly and it will become a thick, creamy frosting.

GELATINE FROSTING.

Soak one teaspoonful of gelatine in one tablespoonful of cold water half an hour, dissolve in two tablespoonfuls of hot water; add one cup of powdered sugar and stir until smooth.

GOLDEN FROSTING.

A very delicious and handsome frosting can be made by using the yolks of eggs instead of the whites. Proceed exactly as for ordinary frosting. It will harden just as nicely as that does. This is particularly good for orange cake, harmonizing with the color of the cake in a way to please those who love rich coloring.

FILLINGS FOR LAYER CAKES.

No. 1. CREAM FILLING.

Cream filling is made with one pint of new milk, two eggs, three tablespoonfuls of sifted flour (or half cup of cornstarch), one cup of sugar. Put two-thirds of the milk on the stove to boil, stir the sugar, flour and eggs in what is left. When the milk boils, put into it the whole and cook it until it is as thick as custard; when cool, add vanilla extract. This custard is nice with a cup of hickory nuts, kernels chopped fine and stirred into it. Spread between the layers of cake. This custard can be made of the yolks of the eggs only, saving the whites for the cake part.

No. 2. ANOTHER CREAM FILLING.

One cup powdered sugar, one-fourth cup hot water. Let them simmer. Beat white of an egg and mix with the above; when cold, add one-half cup chopped raisins, one-half cup chopped walnuts, one tablespoonful of grated cocoanut.

No. 3. ICE-CREAM FILLING.

Make an icing as follows: Three cups of sugar, one of water; boil to a thick, clear syrup, or until it begins to be brittle; pour this, boiling hot, over the *well-beaten* whites of three eggs; stir the mixture very briskly, and pour the sugar in slowly; beat it, when all in, until cool. Flavor with lemon or vanilla extract. This, spread between any white cake layers, answers for "Ice-Cream Cake."

No. 4. APPLE FILLING.

Peel and slice green tart apples, put them on the fire with sugar to suit; when tender, remove, rub them through a fine sieve and add a small piece of butter. When cold, use to spread between the layers; cover the cake with plenty of sugar.

No. 5. ANOTHER APPLE FILLING.

One coffeecup of sugar, one egg, three large apples grated, one lemon grated, juice and outside of the rind; beat together and cook till quite thick. To be cooled before putting on the cake. Spread between layers of cake.

No. 6. CREAM FROSTING.

A cup of sweet thick cream whipped, sweetened and flavored with vanilla; cut a loaf of cake in two, spread the frosting between and on the top; this tastes like Charlotte Russe.

No. 7. PEACH-CREAM FILLING.

Cut peaches into thin slices, or chop them and prepare cream by whipping and sweetening. Put a layer of peaches between the layers of cake and pour cream over each layer and over the top. Bananas, strawberries or other fruits may be used in the same way, mashing strawberries and stewing thick with powdered sugar.

No. 8. CHOCOLATE CREAM FOR FILLING.

Five tablespoonfuls of grated chocolate, enough cream or milk to wet it, one cupful of sugar, one egg, one teaspoonful vanilla flavoring. Stir the ingredients over the fire until thoroughly mixed, having beaten the egg well before adding it; then add the vanilla flavoring after it is removed from the fire.

No. 9. ANOTHER CHOCOLATE FILLING.

The whites of three eggs beaten stiff, one cup of sugar and one cup of grated chocolate, put between the layers and on top.

No. 10. BANANA FILLING.

Make an icing of the whites of two eggs and one cup and a half of powdered sugar. Spread this on the layers, and then cover thickly and entirely with bananas sliced thin or chopped fine. This cake may be flavored with vanilla. The top should be simply frosted.

No. 11. LEMON JELLY FILLING.

Grate the yellow from the rind of two lemons and squeeze out the juice; two cupfuls of sugar, the yolks and whites of two eggs beaten separately. Mix the sugar and yolks, then add the whites and then the lemons. Now pour on a cupful of boiling water; stir into this two tablespoonfuls of sifted flour, rubbed smooth in half a cup of water; then add a tablespoonful of melted butter; cook until it thickens. When cold, spread between the layers of cake. Oranges can be used in place of lemons.

Another filling of lemon (without cooking) is made of the grated rind and juice of two lemons and the whites of two eggs beaten with one cup of sugar.

No. 12. ORANGE CAKE FILLING.

Peel two large oranges, remove the seeds, chop them fine, add half a peeled lemon, one cup of sugar and the well-beaten white of an egg. Spread between the layers of "Silver Cake" recipe.

No. 13. FIG FILLING.

Take a pound of figs, chop fine, and put into a stewpan on the stove; pour over them a teacupful of water and add a half cup of sugar. Cook all together until soft and smooth. When cold spread between layers of cake.

No. 14. FRUIT FILLING.

Four tablespoonfuls of *very finely* chopped citron, four tablespoonfuls of finely chopped seeded raisins, half a cupful of blanched almonds chopped fine, also a quarter of a pound of finely chopped figs. Beat the whites of three eggs to a stiff froth, adding half of a cupful of sugar; then mix thoroughly into this the whole of the chopped ingredients. Put it between the layers of cake when the cake is *hot*, so that it will cook the egg a little. This will be found delicious.

BREAD OR RAISED CAKE.

Two cupfuls of raised dough; beat into it two-thirds of a cup of butter and two cups of sugar creamed together, three eggs, well beaten, one even teaspoonful of soda dissolved in two tablespoonfuls of milk, half a nutmeg grated, one tablespoonful of cinnamon, a teaspoonful of cloves, one cup of raisins. Mix all well together, put in the beaten whites of eggs and raisins last; beat all hard for several minutes; put in buttered pans and let it stand half an hour to rise again before baking. Bake in a *moderate* oven. Half a glass of brandy is an improvement, if you have it convenient.

FRUIT CAKE. (Superior.)

Three pounds dry flour, one pound sweet butter, one pound sugar, three pounds stoned raisins, two pounds currants, three-quarters of a pound sweet almonds blanched, one pound citron, twelve eggs, one tablespoonful allspice, one teaspoonful cloves, two tablespoonfuls cinnamon, two nutmegs, one wine-glass of wine, one wine-glass of brandy, one coffeecupful molasses with the spices in it; steep this gently twenty or thirty minutes, not boiling hot; beat the eggs very lightly; put the fruit in last, stirring it gradually, also a teaspoonful of soda dissolved in a tablespoonful of water; the fruit should be well floured; if necessary add flour after the fruit is in; butter a sheet of paper and lay it in the pan. Lay in some slices of citron, then a layer of the mixture, then of citron again, etc., till the pan is nearly full. Bake three or four hours, according to the thickness of the loaves, in a tolerably hot oven, and with steady heat. Let it cool in the oven gradually. Ice when cold. It improves this cake very much to add three teaspoonfuls of baking powder to the flour. A fine wedding cake recipe.

FRUIT CAKE BY MEASURE, (Excellent.)

Two scant teacupfuls of butter, three cupfuls of dark brown sugar, six eggs, whites and yolks beaten separately, one pound of raisins, seeded, one of currants, washed and dried, and half a pound of citron cut in thin strips; also half a cupful of cooking molasses and half a cupful of sour milk. Stir the butter and sugar to a cream, add to that half a grated nutmeg, ope tablespoonful of ground cinnamon, one teaspoonful of cloves, one teaspoonful of mace, add the molasses and sour milk. Stir all well; then put in the beaten yolks of eggs, a wine-glass of brandy; stir again all thoroughly, and then add four cupfuls of sifted flour alternately with the beaten whites of eggs. Now dissolve a level teaspoonful of soda and stir in thoroughly. Mix the fruit together and stir into it two heaping tablespoonfuls of flour; then stir it in the cake. Butter two common-sized baking tins carefully, line them with letter paper well buttered, and bake in a moderate oven two hours. After it is baked, let it cool in the pan. Afterward put it into a tight can, or let it remain in the pans and cover tightly. Best recipe of all.

WHITE FRUIT CAKE.

One cup of butter, two cups of sugar, one cup of sweet milk, two and one-half cups of flour, the whites of seven eggs, two even teaspoonfuls of baking powder, one pound each of seeded raisins, figs and blanched almonds, and one quarter of a pound of citron, all chopped fine. Mix all thoroughly before adding the fruit; add a teaspoonful of lemon extract. Put baking powder in the flour and mix it well before adding it to the other ingredients. Sift a little flour over the fruit before stirring it in. Bake slowly two hours and try with a splint to see when it is done. A cup of grated cocoanut is a nice addition to this cake.

MOLASSES FRUIT CAKE.

One teacupful of butter, one teacupful of brown sugar, worked well together; next, two teacupfuls of cooking molasses, one cupful of milk with a teaspoonful of soda dissolved in it, one tablespoonful of ginger, one tablespoonful of cinnamon and one teaspoonful of cloves a little grated nutmeg. Now add four eggs well beaten and five cups of sifted flour, or enough to make a stiff batter. Flour a cup of raisins and one of currants; add last. Bake in a very *moderate* oven one hour. If well covered will keep six months.

SPONGE CAKE.

SEPARATE the whites and yolks of six eggs. Beat the yolks to a cream, to which add two teacupfuls of powdered sugar, beating again from five to ten minutes, then add two tablespoonfuls of milk or water, a pinch of salt and flavoring. Now add part of the beaten whites; then two cups of flour in which you have sifted two teaspoonfuls of baking powder; mix gradually into the above ingredients, stirring slowly and lightly, only enough to mix them well; lastly add the remainder of the whites of the eggs. Line the tins with buttered paper and fill two-thirds full.

WHITE SPONGE CAKE.

Whites of five eggs, one cup of flour, one cup sugar, one teaspoonful baking powder; flavor with vanilla. Bake in a quick oven.

ALMOND SPONGE CAKE.

The addition of almonds makes this cake very superior to the usual sponge cake. Sift one pint of fine flour; blanch in scalding water two ounces of sweet and two ounces of bitter almonds, renewing the hot water when expedient; when the skins are all off wash the almonds in cold water (mixing the sweet and bitter) and wipe them dry; pound them to a fine, smooth paste (one at a time), adding, as you proceed, water or white of egg to prevent their boiling. Set them in a cool place; beat ten eggs, the whites and yolks separately, till very smooth and thick, and then beat into them gradually two cups powdered sugar in turn with the pounded almonds; lastly, add the flour, stirring it round slowly and lightly on the surface of the mixture, as in common sponge cake; have ready buttered a *deep* square pan; put the mixture carefully into it, set into the oven and bake till thoroughly done and risen very high; when cool, cover it with plain white icing flavored with rose-water, or with almond icing. With sweet almonds always use a small portion of bitter; without them, *sweet* almonds have little or no taste, though they add to the richness of the cake.

Use two heaping teaspoonfuls of baking powder in the flour.

OLD-FASHIONED SPONGE CAKE.

Two cups of sifted white sugar, two cups of flour measured before sifting, ten eggs. Stir the yolks and sugar together until perfectly light; add a pinch of salt; beat the whites of the eggs to a very stiff froth and add them with the flour, after beating together lightly; flavor with lemon. Bake in a *moderate* oven about forty-five minutes. Baking powder is an improvement to this cake, using two large teaspoonfuls.

LEMON SPONGE CAKE.

Into one level cup of flour put a level teaspoonful of baking powder and sift it. Grate off the yellow rind of a lemon. Separate the whites from the yolks of four eggs. Measure a scant cup of white granulated sugar and beat it to a cream with the yolks, then add the grated rind and a tablespoonful of the juice of the lemon. Stir together until thick and creamy; now beat the whites to a stiff froth; then quickly and lightly mix *without beating* a third of the flour with the yolks; then a third of the whites; then more flour and whites until all are used. The mode of mixing must be very light, rather cutting down through the cake batter than to beating it; beating the eggs makes them light, but beating the batter makes the cake tough. Bake immediately until a straw run into it can be withdrawn clean.

This recipe is especially nice for Charlotte Russe, being so light and porous.

PLAIN SPONGE CAKE.

Beat the yolks of four eggs together with two cups of fine powdered sugar. Stir in gradually one cup of sifted flour and the whites of four eggs beaten to a stiff froth, then a cup of sifted flour in which two teaspoonfuls of baking powder have been stirred, and, lastly, a scant teacupful of boiling water, stirred in a little at a time. Flavor, add salt and, however thin the mixture may seem, do not add any more flour. Bake in shallow tins.

BRIDE'S CAKE.

Cream together one scant cup of butter and three cups of sugar; add one cup of milk, then the beaten whites of twelve eggs; sift three teaspoonfuls of baking powder into one cup of cornstarch mixed with three cups of sifted flour and beat in gradually with the rest; flavor to taste. Beat all thoroughly, then put in buttered tins lined with letter paper well buttered; bake slowly in a *moderate* oven. A beautiful white cake. Ice the top. Double the recipe if more is required.

ENGLISH POUND CAKE.

One pound of butter, one and one-quarter pounds of flour, one pound of pounded loaf sugar, one pound of currants, nine eggs, two ounces of candied peel, one-half ounce of citron, one-half ounce of sweet almonds; when liked, a little pounded mace. Work the butter to a cream; add the sugar, then the well-beaten yolks of eggs, next the flour, currants, candied peel, which should be cut into neat slices, and the almonds, which should be blanched and chopped, and mix all these well together; whisk the whites of eggs and let them be thoroughly blended with the other ingredients. Beat the cake well for twenty minutes and put it into a round tin, lined at the bottom and sides with strips of white buttered paper. Bake it from two hours to two and a half, and let the oven be well heated when the cake is first put in, as, if this is not the case, the currants will all sink to the bottom of it. A glass of wine is usually added to the mixture, but this is scarcely necessary, as the cake will be found quite rich enough without it.

PLAIN POUND CAKE.

This is the old-fashioned recipe that our mothers used to make, and it can be kept for weeks in an earthen jar, closely covered, first dipping letter paper in brandy and placing over the top of the cake before covering the jar.

Beat to a cream one pound of butter with one pound of sugar, after mixing well with the beaten yolks of twelve eggs, one grated nutmeg, one glass of wine, one glass of rose-water. Then stir in one pound of sifted flour and the well-beaten whites of the eggs. Bake a nice light brown.

COCOANUT POUND CAKE.

One-half cupful of butter, two cupfuls of sugar, one cupful of milk, and five eggs, beaten to a stiff froth; one teaspoonful of soda and two of cream of tartar, stirred into four cups of sifted flour. Beat the butter and sugar until very light; to which add the beaten yolks, then the milk, the beaten whites of eggs, then the flour by degrees. After beating all well together, add a small cocoanut grated. Line the cake-pans with paper well buttered, fill rather more than half full and bake in a *moderate* oven. Spread over the top a thin frosting, sprinkled thickly with grated cocoanut.

CITRON POUND CAKE.

Stir two cups of butter to a cream, then beat in the following ingredients each one in succession: one pint of powdered sugar, one quart of flour, a teaspoonful of salt; eight eggs, the yolks and whites beaten separately, and a wine-glass of brandy; then last of all add a quarter of a pound of citron cut into thin slices and floured. Line two cake pans with buttered paper and turn the cake batter in. Bake in a *moderate* oven about three-quarters of an hour.

CITRON CAKE.

Three cups of white sugar and one cup of butter creamed together; one cup of sweet milk, six eggs, whites and yolks beaten separately, one teaspoonful of vanilla or lemon extract, two heaping teaspoonfuls of baking powder, sifted with four cups and a half of flour. One cup and a half of citron, sliced thin and dredged with flour. Divide into two cakes and bake in tins lined with buttered letter paper.

LEMON CAKE.

Three teacupfuls of sugar, one cupful of butter, five eggs, a level teaspoonful of soda dissolved in a cup of sweet milk, four full cups of sifted flour and lastly the grated peel and juice of a lemon, the juice to be added the very last. Bake in two shallow tins. When cold ice with lemon icing and cut into squares.

DELICATE CAKE.

One cup of cornstarch, one of butter, two of sugar, one of sweet milk, two of flour, the whites of seven eggs; rub butter and sugar to a cream; mix one teaspoonful cream of tartar with the flour and cornstarch; one-half teaspoonful soda with the sweet milk; add the milk and soda to the sugar and butter, then add flour, then the whites of eggs; flavor to taste. Never fails to be good.

SILVER, OR DELICATE CAKE.

Whites of six eggs, one cupful of sweet milk, two cupfuls of sugar, four cupfuls of sifted flour, two-thirds of a cup of butter, flavoring and two teaspoonfuls of baking powder. Stir the sugar and butter to a cream, then add the milk and flavoring, part of the flour, the beaten whites of eggs, then the rest of the flour. Bake carefully in tins lined with buttered white paper.

When using the whites of eggs for nice cakes, the yolks need not be wasted; keep them in a cool place and scramble them. Serve on toast or with chipped beef.

GOLD CAKE.

After beating to a cream one cup and a half of butter and two cups of white sugar, stir in the well-whipped yolks of one dozen eggs, four cupfuls of sifted flour, one teaspoonful of baking powder. Flavor with lemon. Line the bake-pans with buttered paper and bake in a moderate oven for one hour.

GOLD OR LEMON CAKE.

Two cups of sugar, half a cup of butter, the yolks of six eggs and one whole one, the grated rind and juice of a lemon or orange, half a teaspoonful of soda dissolved in half a cup of sweet milk, four cups of sifted flour, sifted twice; cream the butter and sugar, then add the beaten yolks and the flour, beating hard for several minutes. Lastly, add the lemon or orange and bake, frosting if liked. This makes a more suitable *lemon* cake than if made with the white parts of eggs added.

SNOW CAKE. (Delicious.)

One pound of arrowroot, quarter of a pound of pounded white sugar, half a pound of butter, the whites of six eggs, flavoring to taste of essence of almonds, or vanilla, or lemon; beat the butter to a cream; stir in the sugar and arrowroot gradually, at the same time beating the mixture; whisk the whites of the eggs to a stiff froth; add them to the other ingredients and beat well for twenty minutes; put in which-ever of the above flavorings may be preferred; pour the cake into a buttered mold or tin and bake it in a *moderate* oven from one to one and a half hours.

MARBLE CAKE.

White Part.—Whites of four eggs, one cup of white sugar, half a cup of butter, half a cup of sweet milk, two teaspoonfuls of baking powder, one teaspoonful of vanilla or lemon and two and a half cups of sifted flour.

Dark Part.—Yolks of four eggs, one cup of brown sugar, half a cup of cooking molasses, half a cup of butter, half a cup of sour milk, one teaspoonful of ground cloves, one teaspoonful of cinnamon, one teaspoonful of mace, one nutmeg grated, one teaspoonful of soda, the soda to be dissolved in a little milk and added after part of the flour is stirred in, one and a half cups of sifted flour.

Drop a spoonful of each kind in a well-buttered cake-dish, first the light part, then the dark, alternately. Try to drop it so that the cake shall be well-streaked through, so that it has the appearance of marble.

SUPERIOR LOAF CAKE.

Two cups of butter, three cups of sugar, two small cups of milk, seven cups of sifted flour; four eggs, the whites and yolks separately beaten; one teacupful of seeded raisins, one teacupful of well-washed and dried currants, one teacupful of sliced citron, one tablespoonful of powdered cinnamon, one teaspoonful of mace, one teaspoonful of soda and one teacupful of home-made yeast.

Take part of the butter and warm it with the milk; stir in part of the flour and the yeast and let it rise; then add the other ingredients with a wine-glass of wine or brandy. Turn all into well-buttered cake-tins and let rise again. Bake slowly in a *moderate* oven for two hours.

FRENCH CHOCOLATE CAKE.

The whites of seven eggs, two cups of sugar, two-thirds of a cup of butter, one cup of milk and three of flour and three teaspoonfuls of baking powder. The chocolate part of the cake is made just the same, only use the yolks of the eggs with a cup of grated chocolate stirred into it. Bake it in layers—the layers being light and dark; then spread a custard between them, which is made with two eggs, one pint of milk, one-half cup of sugar, one tablespoonful of flour or cornstarch; when cool flavor with vanilla, two teaspoonfuls. Fine.

CHOCOLATE CAKE. No. 1.

One cup of butter and two cups of sugar stirred to a cream, with the yolks of five eggs added after they have been well beaten. Then stir into that one cup of milk, beat the whites of two pf the eggs to a stiff froth and add that also; now put in three cups and a half of sifted flour, two heaping teaspoonfuls of baking powder having been stirred into it. Bake in jelly-cake tins.

Mixture for Filling.—Take the remaining three whites of the eggs beaten *very* stiff, two cupfuls of sugar boiled to almost candy or until it becomes stringy or almost brittle; take it hot from the fire and pour it very slowly on the beaten whites of egg, beating quite fast; add one-half cake of grated chocolate, a teaspoonful of vanilla extract. Stir it all until cool, then spread between each cake and over the top and sides. This, when well made, is the *premium* cake of its kind.

CHOCOLATE CAKE. No. 2.

One-half cup butter, two cups sugar, three-quarters of a cup sweet milk, two and one-half cups flour, whites of eight eggs, one teaspoonful of cream of tartar, one-half teaspoonful soda; bake in shallow pans.

For the Frosting.—Take the whites of three eggs, three tablespoonfuls of sugar and one tablespoonful of grated chocolate (confectioners') to one egg; put the cake together with the frosting, then frost the top of the cake with the same.

CHOCOLATE CAKE. No. 3.

Two cups sugar, one cup butter, yolks of five eggs and whites of two and one cup milk. Thoroughly mix two teaspoonfuls baking powder with three and one-half cups flour while dry; then mix all together. Bake in jelly tins.

Mixture for Filling.—Whites of three eggs, one and one-half cups of sugar, three tablespoonfuls of grated chocolate, one teaspoonful of vanilla. Beat together and spread between the layers and on top of the cake.

COCOANUT CAKE.

Cream together three-quarters of a cup of butter and two of white sugar; then add one cup of sweet milk, four eggs, whites and yolks separately beaten, the yolks added first to the butter and sugar, then the whites; flavor with lemon or vanilla; mix three heaping teaspoonfuls of baking powder in three cups of sifted flour and add last; bake in jelly pans.

For Filling.—Make an icing by beating the whites of three eggs and a cup of powdered sugar to a stiff froth. When the cake is cooled, spread a thick layer of this frosting over each cake, and sprinkle very thickly with grated cocoanut.

COCOANUT AND ALMOND CAKE.

Two and one-half cups powdered sugar, one cup butter, four full cups prepared flour, whites of seven eggs whisked stiff, one small cup of milk, with a mere pinch of soda, one grated cocoanut, one-half teaspoonful nutmeg, the juice and half the grated peel of one lemon; cream butter and sugar; stir in lemon and nutmeg; mix well; add the milk and whites and flour alternately. Lastly, stir in the grated cocoanut swiftly and lightly. Bake in four jelly-cake tins.

Filling.—One pound sweet almonds, whites of four eggs whisked stiff, one heaping cup powdered sugar, two teaspoonfuls rose-water. Blanch the almonds. Let them get cold and dry; then pound in a Wedgewood mortar, adding rose-water as you go. Save about two dozen to shred for the top. Stir the paste into the icing after it is made; spread between the cooled cakes; make that for the top a trifle thicker and lay it on heavily. When it has stiffened somewhat, stick the shred almonds closely over it. Set in the oven to harden, but do not let it scorch.

COFFEE CAKE.

One cup of brown sugar, one cup of butter, two eggs, one-half cup of molasses, one cup of strong, cold coffee, one teaspoonful of soda, two teaspoonfuls of cinnamon, one teaspoonful of cloves, one cup of raisins or currants and five cups of sifted flour. Add the fruit last, rubbed in a little of the flour. Bake about one hour.

FEATHER CAKE.

One egg, one cup of sugar, one tablespoonful of cold butter, half a cup of milk, one and one-half cups of flour, one teaspoonful of cream of tartar, half a teaspoonful of soda. A nice plain cake—to be eaten while it is fresh. A spoonful of dried apple sauce or of peach sauce, a spoonful of jelly, the same of lemon extract, nutmeg, cinnamon, cloves and spice —ground—or half a cupful of raisins might be added for a change.

ELECTION CAKE.

Three cups milk, two cups sugar, one cup yeast; stir to a batter and let stand over night; in the morning add two cups sugar, two cups butter, three eggs, half a nutmeg, one tablespoonful cinnamon, one pound raisins, a gill of brandy.

Brown sugar is much better than white for this kind of cake, and it is improved by dissolving a half-teaspoonful of soda in a tablespoonful of milk in the morning. It should stand in the greased pans and rise some time until quite light before baking.

CREAM CAKE.

Four eggs, whites and yolks beaten separately, two teacups of sugar, one cup of sweet cream, two heaping cupfuls of flour, one teaspoonful of soda, mix two teaspoonfuls of cream of tartar in the flour before sifting. Add the whites the last thing before the flour and stir that in gently without beating.

GOLDEN CREAM CAKE.

Yolks of eight eggs beaten to the lightest possible cream, two cupfuls of sugar, a pinch of salt, three teaspoonfuls of baking powder sifted well with flour. Bake in three jelly-cake pans. Make an icing of the whites of three eggs and one pound of sugar. Spread it between the cakes and sprinkle grated cocoanut thickly over each layer. It is delicious when properly made.

DRIED APPLE FRUIT CAKE.

Soak three cupfuls of dried apples over night in cold water enough to swell them; chop them in the morning and put them on the fire with three cups of molasses; stew until almost soft; add a cupful of nice raisins (seedless, if possible) and stew a few moments; when cold, add three cupfuls of flour, one cupful of butter, three eggs and a teaspoonful of soda; bake in a steady oven. This will make two good-sized panfuls of splendid cake; the apples will cook like citron and taste deliciously. Raisins may be omitted; also spices to taste may be added. This is not a dear but a delicious cake.

CAKE WITHOUT EGGS.

Beat together one teacupful of butter and three teacupfuls of sugar, and when quite light stir in one pint of sifted flour. Add to this one pound of raisins seeded and chopped, then mixed with a cup of sifted flour one-teaspoonful of nutmeg, one teaspoonful of powdered cinnamon and lastly one pint of thick sour cream or milk in which a teaspoonful of soda is dissolved. Bake immediately in buttered tins one hour in a *moderate* oven.

WHITE MOUNTAIN CAKE No. 1.

Two cups of sugar, two-thirds cup of butter, the whites of seven eggs well beaten, two-thirds cup of sweet milk, two cups of flour, one cup of cornstarch, two teaspoonfuls baking powder. Bake in jelly-cake tins.

Frosting.—Whites of three eggs and some sugar beaten together not quite as stiff as usual for frosting; spread over the cake, add some grated cocoanut, then put your cakes together; put cocoanut and frosting on top.

WHITE MOUNTAIN CAKE. No. 2.

Cream three cupfuls of sugar and one of butter, making it very light, then add a cupful of milk. Beat the whites of eight eggs very stiff, add half of those to the other ingredients. Mix well into four cups of sifted flour one tablespoonful of baking powder; stir this into the cake, add flavoring, then the remaining beaten whites of egg. Bake in layers like jelly cake. Make an icing for the filling, using the whites of four eggs beaten to a very stiff froth, with two cups of fine white sugar and the juice of half a lemon. Spread each layer of the cake thickly with this icing, place one on another, then ice all over the top and sides. The yolks left from this cake may be used to make a spice cake from the recipe of "Golden Spice Cake."

QUEEN'S CAKE.

Beat well together one cupful of butter and three cupfuls of white sugar, add the yolks of six eggs and one cupful of milk, two teaspoonfuls of vanilla or lemon extract. Mix all thoroughly. To four cupfuls of flour add two heaping teaspoonfuls of cream of tartar and sift gently over the cake stirring all the time. To this add one even teaspoonful of soda dissolved in one tablespoonful of warm water. Mix it well. Stir in gently the whites of six eggs beaten to a stiff foam. Bake slowly. It should be put in the oven as soon as possible after putting in the soda and whites of eggs.

This is the same recipe as the one for "Citron Cake," only omitting the citron.

ANGEL CAKE.

Put into one tumbler of flour one teaspoonful of cream of tartar, then sift it five times. Sift also one glass and a half of white powdered sugar. Beat to a stiff froth the whites of eleven eggs; stir the sugar into the eggs by degrees, very lightly and carefully, adding three teaspoonfuls of vanilla extract. After this add the flour, stirring quickly and lightly. Pour it into a clean, bright tin cake-dish, which should *not* be buttered or lined. Bake at once in a moderate oven about forty minutes, testing it with a broom splint. When done let it remain in the cake-tin, turning it upside down, with the sides resting on the tops of two saucers so that a current of air will pass under and over it.

This is the best recipe found after trying several. A perfection cake.

WASHINGTON LOAF CAKE.

Three cups of sugar, two scant cups of butter, one cup of sour milk, five eggs and one teaspoonful of soda, three tablespoonfuls of cinnamon, half a nutmeg grated and two cups of raisins, one of currants and four cups of sifted flour.

Mix as usual and stir the fruit in at the last, dredged in flour. Line the cake-pans with paper well buttered. This cake will take longer to bake than plain; the heat of the oven must be kept at an even temperature.

MAKING THE PIES.

RIBBON CAKE.

This cake is made from the same recipe as marble cake, only make double the quantity of the white part, and divide it in one-half; put into it a very little cochineal. It will be a delicate pink. Bake in jelly-cake tins and lay first the white, then the dark, then the pink one on top of the others; put together with frosting between. It makes quite a fancy cake. Frost the top when cool.

GOLDEN SPICE CAKE.

This cake can be made to advantage when you have the yolks of eggs left, after having used the whites in making white cake. Take the yolks of seven eggs and one whole egg, two cupfuls of brown sugar, one cupful of molasses, one cupful of butter, one large coffeecupful of sour milk, one teaspoonful of soda (just even full) and five cupfuls of flour, one teaspoonful of ground cloves, two teaspoonfuls of cinnamon, two teaspoonfuls of ginger, one nutmeg and a small pinch of cayenne pepper; beat eggs, sugar and butter to a light batter before putting in the molasses, then add the molasses, flour and milk; beat it well together and bake in a *moderate* oven; if fruit is used, take two cupfuls of raisins, flour them well and put them in last.

ALMOND CAKE.

One-half cupful butter, two cupfuls sugar, four eggs, one-half cupful almonds, blanched—by pouring water on them until skins easily slip off—and cut in fine shreds, one-half teaspoonful extract bitter almonds, one pint flour, one and one-half teaspoonful baking powder, one glass brandy, one-half cupful milk. Rub butter and sugar to a smooth white cream; add eggs, one at a time, beating three or four minutes between each. Sift flour and powder together, add to the butter, etc., with almonds, extract of bitter almonds, brandy and milk; mix into a smooth, medium batter; bake carefully in a rather hot oven twenty minutes.

ROCHESTER JELLY CAKE.

One and one-half cups sugar, two eggs, one-half cup butter, three-fourths cup milk, two heaping cups flour with one teaspoonful cream of tartar, one-half teaspoonful of soda, dissolved in the milk. Put half the above mixture in a small shallow tin, and to the remainder add one teaspoonful molasses, one-half cup raisins (chopped) or currants, one-half teaspoonful cinnamon, cloves, allspice, a little nutmeg and one tablespoonful flour. Bake this in same kind of tins. Put the sheets of cake together, while warm, with jelly between.

FRUIT LAYER CAKE.

This is a delicious novelty in cake-making. Take one cup of sugar, half a cup of butter, one cup and a half of flour, half a cup of wine, one cup of raisins, two eggs and half a teaspoonful of soda; put these ingredients together with care; just as if it were a very rich cake; bake it in three layers and put frosting between—the frosting to be made of the whites of two eggs with enough powdered sugar to make it thick. The top of the cake may be frosted if you choose.

WHIPPED CREAM CAKE.

One cup of sugar and two tablespoonfuls of soft butter stirred together; add the yolks of two eggs well beaten, then add four tablespoonfuls of milk, some flavoring, then the beaten whites of the eggs. Mix a teaspoonful of cream of tartar and half a teaspoon of soda in a cup of flour, sift it into the cake batter and stir lightly. Bake in a small whipping-pan. When the cake is cool, have ready half of a pint of sweet cream sweetened and whipped to a stiff froth, also flavored. Spread it over the cake while fresh. To whip the cream easily, set it on ice before whipping.

ROLLED JELLY CAKE.

Three eggs, one teacup of fine sugar, one teacup of flour; beat the yolks until light, then add the sugar, then add two tablespoonfuls of water, a pinch of salt; lastly stir in the flour, in which there should be a heaping teaspoonful of baking powder. The flour added gradually. Bake in long, shallow biscuit-tins, well greased. Turn out on a damp towel on a bread-board, cover the top with jelly, and roll up while warm.

TO CUT LAYER CAKE.

When cutting Layer Cakes, it is better to first make a round hole in the cake with a knife or tin tube about an inch and a quarter in diameter. This prevents the edge of the cake from crumbling when cutting it.

When making custard filling for Layer Cake always set the dish containing the custard in another dish of boiling water over the fire; this prevents its burning, which would destroy its flavor.

LAYER JELLY CAKE.

Almost any soft cake recipe can be used for jelly cake. The following is excellent: One cup of sugar, half a cup of butter, three eggs, half a cup of sweet milk, two cups of flour, two heaping teaspoonfuls of baking powder, flavoring.

For white, delicate cake the rule for "Silver Cake" is fine; care should be taken, however, that the oven is just right for this cake, as it browns very easily. To be baked in jelly-cake tins in layers, with filling put between when done.

CUSTARD OR CREAM CAKE.

Cream together two cups of sugar and half a cup of butter; add half a cup of sweet milk in which is dissolved half a teaspoonful of soda. Beat the whites of six eggs to a stiff froth and add to the mixture. Have one heaping teaspoonful of cream of tartar stirred thoroughly into three cups of sifted flour and add quickly. Bake in a moderate oven in layers like jelly cake, and, when done, spread custard between.

For the Custard.—Take two cups of sweet milk, put it into a clean suitable dish, set it in a dish of *boiling* water on the range or stove. When the milk comes to a boil add two tablespoonfuls of cornstarch or flour stirred into half a cup of sugar, adding the yolks of four eggs and a little cold milk. Stir this into the boiling milk and when cooked thick enough set aside to cool; afterwards add the flavoring, either vanilla or lemon. It is best to make the custard first, before making the cake part.

HICKORY NUT OR WALNUT CAKE.

Two cups of fine white sugar creamed with half a cup of butter, three eggs, two-thirds of a cup of sweet milk, three cups of sifted flour, one heaping teaspoonful of baking powder sifted through the flour; a tablespoonful (level) of powdered mace, a coffeecup of hickory nut or walnut meats chopped a little. Fill the cake-pans with a layer of the cake, then a layer of raisins upon that, then strew over these a handful of nuts, and so on until the pan is two-thirds full. Line the tins with well-buttered paper and bake in a steady, but not quick, oven. This is most excellent.

CHEAP CREAM CAKE.

One cup of sugar, one egg, one cup sweet milk, two cups flour, one tablespoonful butter, two heaping teaspoonfuls of baking powder; flavor to taste. Divide into three parts and bake in round shallow pans.

Cream.—Beat one egg and one-half cup sugar together, then add one-quarter cup flour, wet with a very little milk and stir this mixture into one-half pint of boiling milk, until thick; flavor to taste. Spread the cream when cool between the cakes.

SOFT GINGER CAKE.

Stir to a cream one cupful of butter and half a cupful of brown sugar; add to this two cupfuls of cooking molasses, a cupful of sweet milk, a tablespoonful of ginger, a teaspoonful of ground cinnamon; beat all thoroughly together, then add three eggs, the whites and yolks beaten separately; beat into this two cups of sifted flour, then a teaspoonful of soda dissolved in a spoonful of water and last, two more cupfuls of sifted flour. Butter and paper two common square bread-pans, divide the mixture and pour half into each. Bake in a moderate oven. This cake requires long and slow baking, from forty to sixty minutes. I find that if sour milk is used the cakes are much lighter, but either sweet or sour is most excellent.

HARD GINGERBREAD.

Made the same as "Soft Gingerbread," omitting the eggs and mixing hard enough to roll out like biscuit; rolled nearly half an inch thick and cut out like small biscuits, or it can be baked in a sheet or on a biscuit-tin; cut slits a quarter of an inch deep across the top of the tin from side to side. When baked and while hot, rub over the top with molasses and let it dry on.

These two recipes are the best I have ever found among a large variety that I have tried, the ingredients giving the best proportion for flavor and excellence.

PLAIN GINGERBREAD.

One cup of *dark* cooking molasses, one cup of sour cream, one teaspoonful of soda dissolved in a little warm water, a teaspoonful of salt and one heaping teaspoonful of ginger; make about as thick as cup cake. To be eaten warm.

WHITE GINGER BISCUIT.

One cup of butter, two cups of sugar, one cup of sour cream or milk, three eggs, one teaspoonful of soda dissolved in a tablespoonful of warm water, one tablespoonful of ginger, one teaspoonful of ground cinnamon and five cups of sifted flour, or enough to roll out *soft*. Cut out rather thick like biscuits; brush over the tops, while hot, with the white of an egg, or sprinkle with sugar while hot.

The grated rind and the juice of an orange add much to the flavor of ginger cake.

GOLD AND SILVER CAKE.

This cake is baked in layers like jelly cake. Divide the silver cake batter and color it pink with a little cochineal; this gives you pink, white and yellow layers. Put together with frosting. Frost the top.

This can be put together like marble cake, first a spoonful of one kind, then another, until the dish is full.

BOSTON CREAM CAKES.

Put into a large-sized saucepan half a cup of butter and one cup of hot water; set it on the fire; when the mixture begins to boil, turn in a pint of sifted flour at once, beat and work it well with a vegetable masher until it is very smooth. Remove from the fire, and when cool enough add five eggs that have been well beaten, first the yolks and then the whites, also half a teaspoonful of soda and a teaspoonful of salt. Drop on buttered tins in large spoonfuls about two inches apart. Bake in a quick oven about fifteen minutes. When done and quite cold, open them on the side with a knife or scissors and put in as much of the custard as possible.

Cream for Filling.—Made of two eggs, three tablespoonfuls of sifted flour (or half cup of cornstarch) and one cup of sugar. Put two-thirds of a pint of milk over the fire in a double boiler; in a third of a pint of milk, stir the sugar, flour and beaten eggs. As soon as the milk looks like boiling, pour in the mixture and stir briskly for three minutes, until it thickens; then remove from the fire and add a teaspoonful of butter; when cool, flavor with vanilla or lemon and fill your cakes.

CHOCOLATE ECLAIRS.

Make the mixture exactly like the recipe for "Boston Cream Cakes." Spread it on buttered pans in oblong pieces about four inches long and one and a half wide, to be laid about two inches apart; they must be baked in a rather quick oven about twenty-five minutes. As soon as baked ice with chocolate icing, and when this is cold split them on one side and fill with the same cream as "Boston Cream Cakes."

HUCKLEBERRY CAKE.

Beat a cup of butter and two cups of sugar together until light, then add a half cup of milk, four eggs beaten separately, the yolks to a cream and the whites to a stiff froth, one teaspoonful of grated nutmeg, the same of cinnamon and two teaspoonfuls of baking powder. The baking powder to be rubbed into the flour. Bub one quart of huckleberries well with some flour and add them last, but do not mash them. Pour into buttered pans, about an inch thick; dust the tops with sugar and bake. It is better the day after baking.

SWEET STRAWBERRY CAKE.

Three eggs, one cupful of sugar, two of flour, one tablespoonful of butter, a teaspoonful, heaped, of baking powder. Beat the butter and sugar together and add the eggs well beaten. Stir in the flour and baking powder well sifted together. Bake in deep tin plate. This quantity will fill four plates. With three pints of strawberries mix a cupful of sugar and mash them a little. Spread the fruit between the layers of cake. The top layer of strawberries may be covered with a meringue made with the white of an egg and a tablespoonful of powdered sugar.

Save out the largest berries and arrange them around in circles on the top in the white frosting. Makes a very fancy dish, as well as a most delicious cake.

MOLASSES CUP CAKES.

One cup of butter, one of sugar, six eggs, five cupfuls of sifted flour, one tablespoonful of cinnamon, two tablespoonfuls of ginger, three teacupfuls of cooking molasses and one heaping teaspoonful of soda. Stir the butter and sugar to a cream; beat the eggs very light, the yolks and whites separately, and add to it; after which put in the spices; then the molasses and flour in rotation, stirring the mixture all the time; beat the whole *well* before adding the soda and but little afterwards. Put into well-buttered patty-pan tins and bake in a *very moderate* oven. A baker's recipe.

BAKERS' GINGER SNAPS.

Boil all together the following ingredients: Two cups of brown sugar, two cups of cooking molasses, one cup of shortening, which should be part butter, one *large* tablespoonful of ginger, one tablespoonful of ground cinnamon, one teaspoonful of cloves; remove from the fire and let it cool. In the meantime, sift four cups of flour and stir part of it into the above mixture. Now dissolve a teaspoonful of soda in a tablespoonful of warm water and beat into this mixture, stir in the remainder of the flour and make stiff enough to roll into long rolls about an inch in diameter, and cut off from the end into half-inch pieces. Place them on well-buttered tins, giving plenty of room to spread. Bake in a moderate oven. Let them cool before taking out of the tins.

GINGER COOKIES.

One cup sugar, one cup molasses, one cup butter, one egg, one tablespoonful vinegar, one tablespoonful ginger, one teaspoonful soda dissolved in boiling water, mix like cooky dough, rather soft.

GINGER SNAPS.

One cup brown sugar, two cups molasses, one large cup butter, two teaspoonfuls soda, two teaspoonfuls ginger, three pints flour to commence with; rub shortening and sugar together into the flour; add enough more flour to roll very smooth, very thin, and bake in a quick oven. The dough can be kept for days by putting it in the flour barrel under the flour, and bake a few at a time. The more flour that can be worked in and the smoother they can be rolled, the better and more brittle they will be. Should be rolled out to wafer-like thinness. Bake quickly without burning. They should become perfectly cold before putting aside.

DOMINOES.

Have a plain cake baked in rather thin sheets and cut into small oblong pieces the size and shape of a domino, a trifle larger. Frost the top and sides. When the frosting is hard, draw the black lines and make the dots with a small brush dipped in melted chocolate. These are very nice for children's parties.

FANCY CAKES.

These delicious little fancy cakes may be made by making a rich jumble-paste—rolling out in any desired shape; cut some paste in thick, narrow strips and lay around your cakes, so as to form a deep, cup-like edge; place on a well-buttered tin and bake. When done, fill with iced fruit prepared as follows: Take rich, ripe peaches (canned ones will do if fine and well drained from all juice) cut in halves; plums, strawberries, pineapples cut in squares or small triangles, or any other available fruit, and dip in the white of an egg that has been very slightly beaten and then in pulverized sugar, and lay in the centre of your cakes.

WAFERS.

Dissolve four ounces of butter in half a teacup of milk; stir together four ounces of white sugar, eight ounces of sifted flour and the yolk of one egg, adding gradually the butter and milk, a tablespoonful of orange-flour water and a pinch of salt; mix it well. Heat the wafer-irons, butter their inner surfaces, put in a tablespoonful of the batter and close the irons immediately; put the irons over the fire, and turn them occasionally, until the wafer is cooked; when the wafers are all cooked roll them on a small round stick, stand them upon a sieve and dry them; serve with ices.

PEACH CAKES.

Take the yolks and whites of five eggs and beat them separately (the whites to a stiff froth.) Then mix the beaten yolks with half a pound of pulverized and sifted loaf or crushed sugar, and beat the two together thoroughly. Fifteen minutes will be none too long for the latter operation if you would have excellence with your cakes.

Now add half a pound of fine flour, dredging it in a little at a time, and then put in the whites of the eggs, beating the whole together for four or five minutes. Then with a large spoon, drop the batter upon a baking tin, which has been buttered and floured, being careful to have the cakes as nearly the same size as possible and resembling in shape the half of a peach. Have a quick oven ready and bake the cakes about ten minutes, watching them closely so that they may only come to a light brown color. Then take them out, spread the flat side of each with peach jam, and stick them together in pairs, covering the outside with a thin coat of icing, which when dry can be brushed over on one side of the cake, with a little cochineal water.

CUP CAKES.

Two cups of sugar, one cup of butter, one cup of milk, three cups and a half of flour and four eggs, half a teaspoonful of soda, large spoon cream of tartar; stir butter and sugar together and add the beaten yolks of the eggs, then the milk, then flavoring and the whites. Put cream of tartar in flour and add last. Bake in buttered gem-pans, or drop the batter, a teaspoonful at a time, in rows on flat buttered tins.

To this recipe may be added a cup of English currants or chopped raisins; and also another variety of cake may be made by adding a half cup citron sliced and floured, a half cupful of chopped almonds and lemon extract.

VARIEGATED CAKES.

One cup powdered sugar, one-half cup of butter creamed with the sugar, one-half cup of milk, four eggs, the whites only, whipped light, two and one-half cups prepared flour. Bitter almond flavoring, spinach juice and cochineal. Cream the butter and sugar; add the milk, flavoring, the whites and flour. Divide the batter into three parts. Bruise and pound a few leaves of spinach in a thin muslin bag until you can express the juice. Put a few drops of this into one portion of the batter, color another with cochineal, leaving the third white. Put a little of each into small, round pans or cups, giving a light stir to each color as you add the next. This will vein the cakes prettily. Put the white between the pink and green, that the tints may show better. If you can get pistachio nuts to pound up for the green, the cakes will be much nicer. Ice on sides and top.

CORNSTARCH CAKES.

One cupful each of butter and sweet milk and half a cup of cornstarch, two cupfuls each of sugar and flour, the whites of five eggs beaten to a stiff froth, two teaspoonfuls of cream of tartar and one of soda; flavor to taste. Bake in gem-tins or patty-pans.

SPONGE DROPS.

Beat to a froth three eggs and one teacup of sugar; stir into this one heaping coffeecup of flour, in which one teaspoonful of cream of tartar and half a teaspoonful of saleratus are thoroughly mixed. Flavor with lemon. Butter tin sheets with washed butter and drop in teaspoonfuls about three inches apart. Bake instantly in a very quick oven. Watch closely as they will burn easily. Serve with ice cream.

SAVORY BISCUITS OR LADY FINGERS.

Put nine tablespoonfuls of fine white sugar into a bowl and put the bowl into hot water to heat the sugar; when the sugar is thoroughly heated, break nine eggs into the bowl and beat them quickly until they become a little warm and rather thick; then take the bowl from the water and continue beating until it is nearly or quite cold; now stir in lightly nine tablespoonfuls of sifted flour; then with a paper funnel, or something of the kind, lay this mixture out upon papers, in biscuits three inches long and half an inch thick, in the form of fingers; sift sugar over the biscuits and bake them upon tins to a light brown; when they are done and cold, remove them from the papers, by wetting them on the back; dry them and they are ready for use. They are often used in making Charlotte Russe.

PASTRY SANDWICHES.

Puff paste, jam of any kind, the white of an egg, sifted sugar.

Roll the paste out thin; put half of it on a baking sheet or tin, and spread equally over it apricot, greengage, or any preserve that may be preferred. Lay over this preserve another thin paste, press the edges together all round, and mark the paste in lines with a knife on the surface, to show where to cut it when baked. Bake from twenty minutes to half an hour; and, a short time before being done, take the pastry out of the oven, brush it over with the white of an egg, sift over pounded sugar and put it back in the oven to color. When cold, cut it into strips; pile these on a dish pyramidically and serve.

This may be made of jelly-cake dough, and, after baking, allowed to cool before spreading with the preserve; either way is good, as well as fanciful.

NEAPOLITAINES.

One cup of powdered sugar, half a cup of butter, two tablespoonfuls of lemon juice, three whole eggs and three yolks, beaten separately, three cups of sifted flour. Put this all together with half a teaspoonful of soda dissolved in a tablespoonful of milk. If it is too stiff to roll out, add just enough more milk. Roll it a quarter of an inch thick and cut it out with any tin cutter. Place the cakes in a pan slightly greased and color the tops with beaten egg and milk, with some chopped almonds over them. Bake in a rather quick oven.

BRUNSWICK JELLY CAKES.

Stir one cup of powdered white sugar and one-half cup of butter together, till perfectly light; beat the yolks of three eggs till very thick and smooth; sift three cups of flour and stir it into the beaten eggs with the butter and sugar; add a teaspoonful of mixed spice (nutmeg, mace and cinnamon) and half a glass of rose-water or wine; stir the whole well and lay it on your paste-board, which must first be sprinkled with flour; if you find it so moist as to be unmanageable, throw in a little more flour; spread the dough into a sheet about half an inch thick and cut it out in round cakes with a biscuit-cutter; lay them in buttered pans and bake about five or six minutes; when cold, spread over the surface of each cake a liquor of fruit jelly or marmalade; then beat the whites of three or four eggs till they stand alone; beat into the froth, by degrees, a sufficiency of powdered loaf sugar to make it as thick as icing; flavor with a few drops of strong essence of lemon, and with a spoon heap it up on each cake, making it high in the centre; put the cakes into a cool oven, and as soon as the tops are colored a pale brown, take them out.

LITTLE PLUM CAKES.

One cup of sugar and half a cup of butter beaten to a smooth cream; add three well-beaten eggs, a teaspoonful of vanilla extract, four cups of sifted flour, one cup of raisins and one of currants, half of a teaspoonful of baking soda dissolved in a little water, and milk enough to make a stiff batter; drop this batter in drops on well-buttered tins and bake in a *quick* oven.

JUMBLES.

Cream together two cups of sugar and one of butter, add three well-beaten eggs and six tablespoonfuls of sweet milk, two teaspoonfuls of baking powder, flavor to taste, flour enough to make into a soft dough; do not roll it on the paste-board, but break off pieces of dough the size of a walnut and make into rings by rolling out rolls as large as your finger, and joining the ends; lay them on tins to bake, an inch apart, as it rises and spreads; bake in a *moderate* oven. These jumbles are very delicate and will keep a long time.

WINE JUMBLES.

One cup of butter, two of sugar, three eggs, one wine-glass of wine, one spoonful of vanilla and flour enough to roll out. Roll as thin as the blade of a knife and cut with an oval cutter. Bake on tin-sheets in a quick oven until a dark brown. These will keep a year if kept in a tin box and in a dry place.

COCOANUT JUMBLES.

Grate one large cupful of cocoanut; rub one cupful of butter with one and a half cupfuls of sugar; add three beaten eggs, whites and yolks separately, two tablespoonfuls of milk and five cupfuls of sifted flour; then add by degrees the grated nut, so as to make a stiff dough, rolled thin and cut with a round cutter, having a hole in the middle. Bake in a quick oven from five to ten minutes.

PHILADELPHIA JUMBLES.

Two cups of sugar, one cup of butter, eight eggs beaten light; essence of bitter almond or rose to taste; enough flour to enable you to roll them out.

Stir the sugar and butter to a light cream, then add the well-whipped eggs, the flavoring and flour; mix well together, roll out in powdered sugar in a sheet a quarter of an inch thick; cut into rings with a jagging-iron and bake in a quick oven on buttered tins.

ALMOND JUMBLES.

Three cupfuls of soft sugar, two cupfuls of flour, half a cupful of butter, one teacupful of loppered milk, five eggs well beaten, two tablespoonfuls of rose-water, three-quarters of a pound of almonds, blanched and chopped *very* fine, one teaspoonful of soda dissolved in boiling water.

Cream butter and sugar; stir in the beaten yolks the milk, flour, rose-water, almonds and, lastly, the beaten whites very lightly and quickly; drop in rings on buttered paper and bake at once.

FRUIT JUMBLES.

Two cups of sugar, one cup of butter, five cupfuls of flour, five eggs, one small teacupful of milk, in which dissolve half a teaspoonful of soda; cream the butter, add the sugar, cream again; then add yolks of eggs, the milk, beaten whites and flour; a little cinnamon, nutmeg, allspice and ground cloves and one-quarter of a pound of currants, rolled in flour.

COOKIES.

One cup of butter, two cups of sugar, a *small* teacupful of sweet milk, half a grated nutmeg and five cups of sifted flour, in which there has been sifted with it two teaspoonfuls of baking powder; mix into a soft dough and cut into round cakes; roll the dough as thin as pie crust. Bake in a quick oven a light brown. These can be made of sour milk and a teaspoonful of soda dissolved in it, or sour or sweet cream can be used in place of butter.

Water cookies made the same as above, using water in place of milk. Water cookies keep longer than milk cookies.

FAVORITE COOKIES.

One cup of butter, one and a half cups of sugar, one-half cup of sour milk one level teaspoonful of soda, a teaspoonful of grated nutmeg Flour enough to roll; make quite soft. Put a tablespoonful of fine sugar on a plate and dip the tops of each as you cut them out. Place on buttered tins and bake in a quick oven a light brown.

FRUIT COOKIES.

One cupful and a half of sugar, one cupful of butter, one-half cup of sweet milk, one egg, two teaspoonfuls of baking powder, a teaspoonful of grated nutmeg, three tablespoonfuls of English currants or chopped raisins. Mix soft and roll out, using just enough flour to stiffen sufficiently. Cut out with a large cutter, wet the tops with milk and sprinkle sugar over them. Bake on buttered tins in a quick oven.

CRISP COOKIES. (Very Nice.)

One cup of butter, two cups of sugar, three eggs well beaten, a teaspoonful of soda and two of cream of tartar, spoonful of milk, one teaspoonful of nutmeg and one of cinnamon. Flour enough to make a soft dough just stiff enough to roll out. Try a pint of sifted flour to begin with, working it in gradually. Spread a little sweet milk over each and sprinkle with sugar. Bake in a quick oven a light brown.

LEMON COOKIES.

Four cups of sifted flour, or enough for a stiff dough, one teacupful of butter, two cups of sugar, the juice of one lemon and the grated peel from the outside, three eggs whipped very light. Beat thoroughly each ingredient, adding, after all is in, a half teaspoonful of soda dissolved in a tablespoonful of milk. Roll out as any cookies and bake a light brown. Use no other wetting.

COCOANUT COOKIES.

One cup grated cocoanut, one and one-half cups sugar, three-fourths cup butter, one-half cup milk, two eggs, one large teaspoonful baking powder, one-half teaspoonful extract of vanilla and flour enough to roll out.

DOUGHNUTS OR FRIED CAKES.

Success in making good fried cakes depends as much on the *cooking* as the mixing. In the first place, there should be boiling lard enough to free them from the bottom of the kettle, so that they swim on the top, and the lard should never be so hot as to smoke or so cool as not to be at the boiling point; if it is, they soak grease and are spoiled. If it is at the right heat, the doughnuts will in about ten minutes be of a delicate brown outside and nicely cooked inside. Five or six minutes will cook a cruller. Try the fat by dropping a bit of the dough in first; if it is right, the fat will boil up when it is dropped in. They should be turned over almost constantly, which causes them to rise and brown evenly. When they are sufficiently cooked, raise them from the hot fat and drain them until every drop ceases dripping.

CRULLERS OR FRIED CAKES.

One and a half cupfuls of sugar, one cupful of sour milk, two eggs, two scant tablespoonfuls of melted butter, half a nutmeg grated, a large teaspoonful of cinnamon, a teaspoonful of salt and one of soda; make a little stiffer than biscuit dough, roll out a quarter of an inch thick, and cut with a fried-cake cutter, with a hole in the centre. Fry in hot lard.

These can be made with sweet milk and baking powder, using two heaping teaspoonfuls of the baking powder in place of soda.

RAISED DOUGHNUTS.

Old-fashioned "raised doughnuts" are seldom seen nowadays, but are easily made. Make a sponge as for bread, using a pint of warm water or milk, and a large half cupful of yeast; when the sponge is very light, add half a cupful of butter or sweet lard, a coffeecupful of sugar, a teaspoonful of salt and one small teaspoonful of soda dissolved in a little water, one tablespoonful of cinnamon, a little grated nutmeg; stir in now two well-beaten eggs, add sifted flour until it is the consistency of biscuit dough, knead it well, cover and let rise; then roll the dough out into a sheet half an inch thick, cut out with a very small biscuit-cutter, or in strips half an inch wide and three inches long, place them on greased tins, cover them well and let them rise before frying them. Drop them in very hot lard. Raised cakes require longer time than cakes made with baking powder. Sift powdered sugar over them as fast as they are fried, while warm. Our grandmothers put allspice into these cakes; that, however, is a matter of taste.

BAKERS' RAISED DOUGHNUTS.

Warm a teacupful of lard in a pint of milk; when nearly cool add enough flour to make a thick batter and add a small cupful of yeast; beat it well and set it to rise; when light work in gradually and carefully three cupfuls of sugar, the whipped whites of six eggs, half a teaspoonful of soda dissolved in a spoonful of milk, one teaspoonful of salt, a teaspoonful of ground cinnamon and half of a nutmeg grated; then work in gradually enough flour to make it stiff enough to roll out; let it rise again and when very light roll it out in a sheet an inch thick; cut into rounds; put into the centre of each round a large Sultana raisin, seeded, and mold into perfectly round balls; flatten a little; let them stand a few minutes before boiling them; have plenty of lard in the pot and when it boils drop in the cakes; when they are a light, brown take them out with a perforated skimmer; drain on soft white paper and roll, while warm, in fine powdered sugar.

CRULLERS OR WONDERS.

Three eggs, three tablespoonfuls of melted lard or butter, three tablespoonfuls of sugar; mix very hard with sifted flour, as hard as can be rolled, and to be rolled very thin like pie crust; cut in squares three inches long and two wide, then cut several slits or lines lengthwise to within a quarter of an inch of the edges of the ends; run your two forefingers through every other slit; lay them down on the board edgewise and dent them. These are very dainty when fried. Fry in hot lard a light brown.

GERMAN DOUGHNUTS.

One pint of milk; four eggs, one small tablespoonful of melted butter, flavoring, salt to taste; first boil the milk and pour it, while hot, over a pint of flour; beat it very smooth and when it is cool have ready the yolks of the eggs well beaten; add them to the milk and flour, beaten well into it, then add the well-beaten whites; then, lastly, add the salt and as much more flour as will make the whole into a soft dough; flour your board, turn your dough upon it, roll it in pieces as thick as your finger and turn them in the form of a ring; cook in plenty of boiling lard. A nice breakfast cake with coffee.

CUTTING PUMPKIN FOR PIES.

NUT CAKES. (Fried.)

Beat two eggs well, add to them one ounce of sifted sugar, two ounces of warmed butter, two tablespoonfuls of yeast, a teacupful of luke-warm milk and a little salt. Whip all well together, then stir in by degrees one pound of flour, and, if requisite, more milk, making thin dough. Beat it until it falls from the spoon, then set it to rise. When it has risen make butter or lard hot in a frying pan, cut from the light dough little pieces the size of a walnut, and, without molding or kneading, fry them pale brown. As they are done lay them on a napkin to absorb any of the fat.

TRIFLES.

Work one egg and a tablespoonful of sugar to as much flour as will make a stiff paste; roll it as thin as a dollar piece and cut it into small round or square cakes; drop two or three at a time into the boiling lard; when they rise to the surface and turn over they are done; take them out with a skimmer and lay them on an inverted sieve to drain. When served for dessert or supper put a spoonful of jelly on each.

PUFF-BALL DOUGHNUTS.

These doughnuts, eaten fresh and warm, are a delicious breakfast dish and are quickly made. Three eggs, one cupful of sugar, a pint of sweet milk, salt, nutmeg and flour enough to permit the spoon to stand upright in the mixture; add two heaping teaspoonfuls of baking powder to the flour; beat all until very light. Drop by the dessertspoonful into boiling lard. These will not absorb a bit of fat and are not at all rich and consequently are the least injurious of this kind of cakes.

PASTRY, PIES AND TARTS.

GENERAL REMARKS.

Use the very best materials in making pastry; the shortening should be fresh, sweet and hard; the water cold (ice-water is best), the paste rolled on a cold board and all handled as little as possible. When the crust is made, it makes it much more flaky and puff much more to put it in a dish covered with a cloth and set in a very cold place for half an hour, or even an hour; in summer, it could be placed in the ice box.

A great improvement is made in pie crust by the addition of about a heaping teaspoonful of baking powder to a quart of flour, also brushing the paste as often as rolled out, and the pieces of butter placed thereon, with the white of an egg, assists it to rise in *leaves* or *flakes*. As this is the great beauty of puff paste, it is as well to try this method.

If currants are to be used in pies, they should be carefully picked over and washed in several waters, dried in a towel and dredged with flour before they are suitable for use.

Raisins, and all dried fruits for pies and cakes, should be seeded stoned and dredged with flour before using.

Almonds should be blanched by pouring boiling water upon them and then slipping the skin off with the fingers. In pounding them, always add a little rose or orange-water, with fine sugar, to prevent their becoming oily.

Great care is requisite in heating an oven for baking pastry. If you can hold your hand in the heated oven while you count twenty, the oven has just the proper temperature and it should be kept at this temperature as long as the pastry is in; this heat will bake to a light brown and will give the pastry a fresh and flaky appearance. If you suffer the heat to abate, the under crust will become heavy and clammy and the upper crust will fall in.

Another good way to ascertain when the oven is heated to the proper degree for puff paste: put a small piece of the paste in previous to baking the whole, and then the heat can thus be judged of.

Pie crust can be kept a week, and the last be better than the if put in a tightly covered dish and set in the ice chest in summer and in a cool place in winter, and thus you can make a fresh pie every day with little trouble.

In baking custard, pumpkin or squash pies, it is well, in order that the mixture may not be absorbed by the paste, to first partly bake the paste before adding it, and when stewed fruit is used the filling should be perfectly cool when put in, or it will make the bottom crust sodden.

HOW TO MAKE A PIE.

After making the crust, take a portion of it, roll it out and fit it to a buttered pie-plate by cutting it off evenly around the edge; gather up the scraps left from cutting and make into another sheet for the top crust; roll it a little thinner than the under crust; lap one-half over the other and cut three or four slits about a quarter of an inch from the folded edge (this prevents the steam from escaping through the rim of the pie, and causing the juices to run out from the edges). Now fill your pie-plate with your prepared filling, wet the top edge of the rim, lay the upper crust across the centre of the pie, turn back the half that is lapped over, seal the two edges together by slightly pressing down with your thumb, then notch evenly and regularly with a three-tined fork, dipping occasionally in flour to prevent sticking. Bake in a rather quick oven a light brown, and until the filling boils up through the slits in the upper crust.

To prevent the juice soaking through into the crust, making it soggy wet the under crust with the white of an egg, just before you put in the pie mixture. If the top of the pie is brushed over with the egg, it gives it a beautiful glaze.

FOR ICING PASTRY.

To ice pastry, which is the usual method adopted for fruit tarts and sweet dishes of pastry, put the white of an egg on a plate and with the blade of a knife beat it to a stiff froth. When the pastry is nearly baked, brush it over with this and sift over some pounded sugar; put it back into the oven to set the glaze and in a few minutes it will be done. Great care should be taken that the paste does not catch or burn in the oven, which is very liable to do after the icing is laid on.

Or make a meringue by adding a tablespoonful of white sugar to the beaten white of one egg. Spread over the top and slightly brown in the oven.

FINE PUFF PASTE.

Into one quart of sifted flour mix two teaspoonfuls of baking powder and a teaspoonful of salt; *then sift again*. Measure out one teacupful of butter and one of lard, hard and cold. Take the lard and rub into the flour until a very fine smooth paste. Then put in just enough *ice-water*, say half a cupful, containing a beaten white of egg, to mix a very stiff dough. Boll it out into a thin sheet, spread with one-fourth of the butter, sprinkle over with a little flour, then roll up closely in a long roll, like a scroll, double the ends towards the centre, flatten and re-roll, then spread again with another quarter of the butter. Repeat this operation until the butter is used up. Put it on an earthen dish, cover it with a cloth and set it in a cold place, in the ice box in summer; let it remain until *cold*; an hour or more before making out the crust. Tarts made with this paste cannot be cut with a knife when fresh; they go into flakes at the touch.

You may roll this pastry in any direction, from you, toward you, sideways, any way, it matters not, but you must have nice flour, *ice-water* and very *little* of it, and strength to roll it, if you would succeed.

This recipe I purchased from a colored cook on one of the Lake Michigan steamers many years ago, and it is, without exception, the finest puff paste I have ever seen.

PUFF PASTE FOR PIES.

One quart of pastry flour, one pint of butter, one tablespoonful of salt, one of sugar, one and a quarter cupfuls of ice-water. Wash the hands with soap and water and dip them first in very hot and then in cold water. Rinse a large bowl or pan with boiling water and then with cold. Half fill it with cold water. Wash the butter in this, working it with the hands until it is light and waxy. This frees it from the salt and buttermilk and lightens it, so that the pastry is more delicate. Shape the butter into two thin cakes and put in a pan of ice-water to harden. Mix the salt and sugar with the flour. With the hands, rub one-third of the butter into the flour. Add the water, stirring with a knife. Stir quickly and vigorously until the paste is a smooth ball. Sprinkle the board *lightly* with flour. Turn the paste on this and pound quickly and lightly with the rolling-pin. Do not break the paste. Roll from you and to one side; or if easier to roll from you all the time, turn the paste around. When it is about one-fourth of an inch thick, wipe the remaining butter, break it in bits and spread these on the paste. Sprinkle lightly with flour. Fold the paste, one-third from each side, so that the edges meet. Now fold from the ends, but do not have these meet. Double the paste, pound lightly and roll down to about one-third of an inch in thickness. Fold as before and roll down again. Repeat this three times if for pies and six times if for *vol-au-vents*, patties, tarts, etc. Place on the ice to harden, when it has been rolled the last time. It should be in the ice chest at least an hour before being used. In hot weather, if the paste sticks when being rolled down, put it on a tin sheet and place on ice. As soon as it is chilled, it will roll easily. The less flour you use in rolling out the paste, the tenderer it will be. No matter how carefully every part of the work may be done, the paste will not be good if much flour is used.

SOYER'S RECIPE FOR PUFF PASTE.

To every pound of flour allow the yolk of one egg, the juice of one lemon, half a saltspoonful of salt, cold water, one pound of fresh butter.

Put the flour onto the paste-board; make a hole in the centre, into which put the yolk of the egg, the lemon juice and salt; mix the whole with cold water (this should be iced in summer if convenient) into a soft, flexible paste with the right hand, and handle it as little as possible; then squeeze all the buttermilk from the butter, wring it in a cloth and roll out the paste; place the butter on this and fold the edges of the paste over, so as to hide it; roll it out again to the thickness of a quarter of an inch; fold over one-third, over which again pass the rolling-pin; then fold over the other third, thus forming a square; place it with the ends, top and bottom before you, shaking a little flour both under and over, and repeat the rolls and turns twice again as before. Flour a baking-sheet, put the paste on this and let it remain on ice or in some cool place for half an hour; then roll twice more, turning it as before; place it again upon the ice for a quarter of an hour, give it two more rolls, making seven in all, and it is ready for use when required.

RULE FOR UNDER CRUST.

A good rule for pie crust for a pie requiring only an under crust, as a custard or pumpkin pie, is: Three *large* tablespoonfuls of flour sifted, rubbing into it a *large* tablespoonful of cold butter, or part butter and part lard, and a pinch of salt, mixing with *cold* water enough to form a smooth, stiff paste, and rolled quite thin.

PLAIN PIE CRUST.

Two and a half cupfuls of sifted flour, one cupful of shortening, half butter and half lard cold, a pinch of salt, a heaping teaspoonful of baking powder sifted through the flour. Rub thoroughly the shortening into the flour. Mix together with half a teacupful of *cold* water, or enough to form a rather stiff dough; mix as little as possible, just enough to get it into shape to roll out; it must be handled very lightly. This rule is for two pies.

When you have a little pie crust left do not throw it away; roll it thin, cut in small squares and bake. Just before tea put a spoonful of raspberry jelly on each square.

PUFF PASTE OF SUET.

Two cupfuls of flour, one-half teaspoonful of salt, one teaspoonful of baking powder, one cup of chopped suet, freed of skin, and chopped very fine, one cupful of water. Place the flour, sifted with the powder in a bowl, add suet and water; mix into smooth, rather firm dough.

This paste is excellent for fruit puddings and dumplings that are boiled; if it is well made, it will be light and flaky and the suet impreceptible. It is also excellent for meat pies, baked or boiled. All the ingredients should be very cold when mixing, and the suet dredged with flour after it is chopped, to prevent the particles from adhering to each other.

POTATO CRUST.

Boil and mash a dozen medium-sized potatoes, add one good teaspoonful of salt, two tablespoonfuls of cold butter and half a cupful of milk or cream. Stiffen with flour sufficient to roll out. Nice for the tops of meat pies.

TO MAKE PIE CRUST FLAKY.

In making a pie, after you have rolled out your top crust, cut it about the right size, spread it over with butter, then shake sifted flour over the butter, enough to cover it well. Cut a slit in the middle place it over the top of your pie, and fasten the edges as any pie. Now take the pie on your left hand and a dipper of cold water in your right hand; tip the pie slanting a little, pour over the water sufficiently to rinse off the flour. Enough flour will stick to the butter to fry into the crust, to give it a fine, blistered, flaky look, which many cooks think is much better than rolling the butter into the crust.

TARTLETS. No. 1.

Tarts of strawberry or any other kind of preserves are generally made of the trimmings of puff paste rolled a little thicker than the ordinary pies; then cut out with a round cutter, first dipped in hot water, to make the edges smooth, and placed in small tart-pans, first pricking a few holes at the bottom with a fork before placing them in the oven. Bake from ten to fifteen minutes. Let the paste cool a little; then fill it with preserve. By this manner, both the flavor and color of the jam are preserved, which would be lost were it baked in the oven on the paste; and, besides, so much jam is not required.

TARTLETS. No. 2.

Tartlets are nice made in this manner: Roll some good puff paste out thin, and cut it into two and a half inch squares; brush each square over with the white of an egg, then fold down the corners, so that they all meet in the middle of each piece of paste; slightly press the two pieces together, brush them over with the egg, sift over sugar and bake in a nice quick oven for about a quarter of an hour. When they are done, make a little hole in the middle of the paste and fill it up with apricot jam, marmalade, or red currant jelly. Pile them high in the centre of a dish on a napkin and garnish with the same preserves the tartlets are filled with.

PATTIES, OR SHELLS FOR TARTS.

Roll out a nice puff paste thin; cut out with a glass or cookie-cutter and with a wine-glass or smaller cutter, cut out the centre of two out of three; lay the rings thus made on the third, and bake at once. May be used for veal or oyster patties, or filled with jelly, jam or preserves, as tarts. Or shells may be made by lining patty-pans with paste. If the paste is light, the shells will be fine. Filled with jelly and covered with meringue (tablespoonful of sugar to the white of one egg) and browned in oven, they are very nice to serve for tea.

If the cutters are dipped in *hot water*, the edges of the tartlets will rise much higher and smoother when baking.

TARTS.

Larger pans are required for tarts proper, the size of small, shallow pie-tins; then after the paste is baked and cooled and filled with the jam or preserve, a few stars or leaves are placed on the top, or strips of paste, criss-crossed on the top, all of which have been previously baked on a tin by themselves.

Dried fruit, stewed until thick, makes fine tart pies, also cranberries stewed and well sweetened.

GREEN APPLE PIE.

Peel, core and slice tart apples enough for a pie; sprinkle over about three tablespoonfuls of sugar, a teaspoonful of cinnamon, a small level tablespoonful of sifted flour, two tablespoonfuls of water, a few bits of butter, stir all together with a spoon; put it into a pie-tin lined with pie paste; cover with a top crust and bake about forty minutes.

The result will be a delicious, juicy pie.

APPLE CUSTARD PIE. No. 1.

Three cupfuls of milk, four eggs and one cupful of sugar, two cupfuls of thick stewed apples, strained through a colander. Beat the whites and yolks of the eggs lightly and mix the yolks well with the apples, flavoring with nutmeg. Then beat into this the milk and, lastly, the whites. Let the crust partly bake before turning in this filling. To be baked with only the one crust, like all custard pies.

APPLE CUSTARD PIE. No. 2.

Select fair sweet apples, pare and grate them, and to every teacupful of the apple add two eggs well beaten, two tablespoonfuls of fine sugar, one of melted butter, the grated rind and half the juice of one lemon, half a wine-glass of brandy and one teacupful of milk; mix all well and pour into a deep plate lined with paste; put a strip of the paste around the edge of the dish and bake thirty minutes.

APPLE CUSTARD PIE. No. 3.

Lay a crust in your plates; slice apples thin and half fill your plates; pour over them a custard made of four eggs and one quart of milk, sweetened and seasoned to your taste.

APPLE CUSTARD PIE. No. 4.

Peel sour apples and stew until soft, and not much water left in them; then rub through a colander; beat three eggs for each pie to be baked and put in at the rate of one cupful of butter and one of sugar for three pies; season with nutmeg.

IRISH APPLE PIE.

Pare and take out the cores of the apples, cutting each apple into four or eight pieces, according to their size. Lay them neatly in a baking dish, seasoning them with brown sugar and any spice, such as pounded cloves and cinnamon, or grated lemon peel. A little quince marmalade gives a fine flavor to the pie. Add a little water and cover with puff paste. Bake for an hour.

MOCK APPLE PIE.

Crush finely with a rolling pin, one large Boston cracker; put it into a bowl and pour upon it one teacupful of cold water; add one teacupful of fine white sugar, the juice and pulp of one lemon, half a lemon rind grated and a little nutmeg; line the pie-plate with half puff paste, pour in the mixture, cover with the paste and bake half an hour.

These are proportions for one pie.

APPLE AND PEACH MERINGUE PIE.

Stew the apples or peaches and sweeten to taste. Mash smooth and season with nutmeg. Fill the crusts and bake until just done. Put on no top crust. Take the whites of three eggs for each pie and whip to a stiff froth, and sweeten with three tablespoonfuls of powdered sugar. Flavor with rose-water or vanilla; beat until it will stand alone; then spread it on the pie one-half to one inch thick; set it back into the oven until the meringue is well "set." Eat cold.

COCOANUT PIE. No. 1.

One-half cup desiccated cocoanut soaked in one cupful of milk, two eggs, one small cupful of sugar, butter the size of an egg. This is for one small-sized pie. Nice with a meringue on top.

COCOANUT PIE. No. 2.

Cut off the brown part of the cocoanut, grate the white part, mix it with milk and set it on the fire and let it boil slowly eight or ten minutes. To a pound of the grated cocoanut, allow a quart of milk, eight eggs, four tablespoonfuls of sifted white sugar, a glass of wine, a small cracker, pounded fine, two spoonfuls of melted butter and half a nutmeg. The eggs and sugar should be beaten together to a froth, then the wine stirred in. Put them into the milk and cocoanut, which should be first allowed to get quite cool; add the cracker and nutmeg, turn the whole into deep pie plates, with a lining and rim of puff paste. Bake them as soon as turned into the plates.

CHOCOLATE CUSTARD PIE. No. 1.

One-quarter cake of Baker's chocolate, grated; one pint of boiling water, six eggs, one quart of milk, one-half cupful of white sugar, two teaspoonfuls of vanilla. Dissolve the chocolate in a very little milk, stir into the boiling water and boil three minutes. When nearly cold beat up with this the yolks of all the eggs and the whites of three. Stir this mixture into the milk, season and pour into shells of good paste. When the custard is "set"—but not more than half done—spread over it the whites whipped to a froth, with two tablespoonfuls of sugar. You may bake these custards without paste, in a pudding dish or cups set in boiling water.

CHOCOLATE PIE. No. 2.

Put some grated chocolate into a basin and place on the back of the stove and let it melt (do not add any water to it); beat one egg and some sugar in it; when melted, spread this on the top of a custard pie. Lovers of chocolate will like this.

LEMON PIE. No. 1. (Superior.)

Take a deep dish, grate into it the outside of the rind of two lemons; add to that a cup and a half of white sugar, two heaping tablespoonfuls of unsifted flour, or one of cornstarch; stir it well together, then add the yolks of three well-beaten eggs, beat this thoroughly, then add the juice of the lemons, two cups of water and a piece of butter the size of a walnut. Set this on the fire in another dish containing boiling water and cook it until it thickens, and will dip up on the spoon like cold honey. Remove from the fire, and when cooled, pour it into a deep pie-tin, lined with pastry; bake, and when done, have ready the whites, beaten stiff, with three small tablespoonfuls of sugar. Spread this over the top and return to the oven, to set and brown slightly. This makes a deep, large sized pie, and very superior.

LEMON PIE. No. 2.

One coffee cupful of sugar, three eggs, one cupful of water, one tablespoonful of melted butter, one heaping tablespoonful of flour, the juice and a little of the rind of one lemon. Reserve the whites of the eggs, and after the pie is baked, spread them over the top beaten lightly-with a spoonful of sugar, and return to the oven until it is a light brown.

This may be cooked before it is put into the crust or not, but it is rather better to cook it first in a double boiler or dish. It makes a medium-sized pie. Bake from thirty-five to forty minutes.

LEMON PIE. No. 3.

Moisten a heaping tablespoonful of cornstarch with a little cold water, then add a cupful of boiling water; stir over the fire till it boils and cook the cornstarch, say two or three minutes; add teaspoonful of butter and a cupful of sugar; take off the fire and, when slightly cooled, add an egg well beaten and the juice and grated rind of a fresh lemon. Bake with a crust. This makes one small pie.

LEMON PIE. No. 4.

Two large, fresh lemons, grate off the rind, if not bitter reserve it for the filling of the pie, pare off every bit of the white skin of the lemon (as it toughens while cooking); then cut the lemon into very thin slices with a sharp knife and take out the seeds; two cupfuls of sugar, three tablespoonfuls of water and two of sifted flour. Put into the pie a layer of lemon, then one of sugar, then one of the grated rind and, lastly, of flour, and so on till the ingredients are used; sprinkle the water over all, and cover with upper crust. Be sure to have the under crust lap over the upper, and pinch it well, as the syrup will cook all out if care is not taken when finishing the edge of crust. This quantity makes one medium-sized pie.

ORANGE PIE.

Grate the rind of one and use the juice of two large oranges. Stir together a large cupful of sugar and a heaping tablespoonful of flour; add to this the well-beaten yolks of three eggs, two tablespoonfuls of melted butter. Reserve the whites for frosting. Turn this into a pie-pan lined with pie paste and bake in a quick oven. When done so as to resemble a finely baked custard, spread on the top of it the beaten whites, which must be sweetened with two tablespoonfuls of sugar; spread evenly and return to the oven and brown slightly.

The addition of the juice of half a lemon improves it, if convenient to have it.

BAKERS' CUSTARD PIE.

Beat up the yolks of three eggs to a cream. Stir thoroughly a tablespoonful of sifted flour into three tablespoonfuls of sugar; this separates the particles of flour so that there will be no lumps; then add it to the beaten yolks, put in a pinch of salt, a teaspoonful of vanilla and a little grated nutmeg; next the well-beaten whites of the eggs; and, lastly, a pint of scalded milk (not boiled) which has been cooled; mix this in by degrees and turn all into a deep pie-pan lined with puff paste, and bake from twenty-five to thirty minutes.

I received this recipe from a celebrated cook in one of our best New York bakeries. I inquired of him "why it was that their custard pies had that look of solidity and smoothness that our home-made pies have not." He replied, "The secret is the addition of this *bit of flour*—not that it thickens the custard any to speak of, but prevents the custard from breaking or wheying and gives that smooth appearance when cut."

CREAM PIE.

Pour a pint of cream upon one and a half cupfuls of sugar; let it stand until the whites of three eggs have been beaten to a stiff froth; add this to the cream and beat up thoroughly; grate a little nutmeg over the mixture and bake without an upper crust. If a tablespoonful of sifted flour is added to it, as the above Custard Pie recipe, it would improve it.

WHIPPED CREAM PIE.

Line a pie plate with a rich crust and bake quickly in a hot oven. When done, spread with a thin layer of jelly or jam, then whip one cupful of thick sweet cream until it is as light as possible; sweeten with powdered sugar and flavor with vanilla; spread over the jelly or jam; set the cream where it will get very cold before whipping.

CUSTARD PIE.

Beat together until very light the yolks of four eggs and four tablespoonfuls of sugar, flavor with nutmeg or vanilla; then add the four beaten whites, a pinch of salt and, lastly, a quart of sweet milk; mix well and pour into tins lined with paste. Bake until firm.

BOSTON CREAM PIE.

Cream Part.—Put on a pint of milk to boil. Break two eggs into a dish and add one cup of sugar and half a cup of flour previously mixed after beating well, stir it into the milk just as the milk commences to boil; add an ounce of butter and keep on stirring one way until it thickens; flavor with vanilla or lemon.

Crust Part.—Three eggs beaten separately, one cup of granulated sugar, one and a half cups of sifted flour, one large teaspoonful of baking powder and two tablespoonfuls of milk or water. Divide the batter in half and bake on two medium-sized pie-tins. Bake in a rather quick oven to a straw color. When done and cool, split each one in half with a sharp broad-bladed knife, and spread half the cream between each. Serve cold.

The cake part should be flavored the same as the custard.

MOCK CREAM PIE.

Take three eggs, one pint of milk, a cupful of sugar, two tablespoonfuls of cornstarch or three of flour; beat the sugar, cornstarch and yolks of the eggs together; after the milk has come to a boil, stir in the mixture and add a pinch of salt and about a teaspoonful of butter. Make crust the same as any pie; bake, then fill with the custard, grate over a little nutmeg and bake again. Take the whites of the eggs and beat to a stiff froth with two tablespoonfuls of sugar, spread over the top and brown in a quick oven.

FRUIT CUSTARD PIE.

Any fruit custard, such as pineapple, banana, can be readily made after the recipe of APPLE CUSTARD PIE.

CHERRY PIE.

Line your pie plate with good crust, fill half full with ripe cherries; sprinkle over them about a cupful of sugar, a teaspoonful of sifted flour, dot a few bits of butter over that. Now fill the crust full to the top. Cover with the upper crust and bake.

This is one of the best of pies, if made correctly, and the cherries in any case should be stoned.

CURRANT PIE.

Make in just the same way as the "Cherry Pie," unless they are somewhat green, then they should be stewed a little.

RIPE CURRANT PIE.

One cupful of mashed ripe currants, one of sugar, two tablespoonfuls of water, one of flour, beaten with the yolks of two eggs. Bake; frost the top with the beaten whites of the eggs and two tablespoonfuls powdered sugar and brown in oven.

GREEN TOMATO PIE.

Take medium-sized tomatoes, pare and cut out the stem end. Having your pie-pan lined with paste made as biscuit dough, slice the tomatoes *very thin*, filling the pan somewhat heaping, then grate over it a nutmeg; put in half a cup of butter and a medium cup of sugar, if the pan is rather deep. Sprinkle a small handful of flour over all, pouring in half a cup of vinegar before adding the top crust. Bake half an hour in a moderately hot oven, serving hot. Is good; try it.

APRICOT MERINGUE PIE.

A canned apricot meringue pie is made by cutting the apricots fine and mixing them with half a cup of sugar and the beaten yolk of an egg; fill the crust and bake. Take from the oven, let it stand for two or three minutes, cover with a meringue made of the beaten white of an egg and one tablespoonful of sugar. Set back in a slow oven until it turns a golden brown. The above pie can be made into a tart without the addition of the meringue by adding criss-cross strips of pastry when the pie is first put into the oven.

All of the above are good if made from the dried and stewed apricots instead of the canned and are much cheaper.

Stewed dried apricots are a delicious addition to mince meat. They may be used in connection with minced apples, or to the exclusion of the latter.

HUCKLEBERRY PIE.

Put a quart of picked huckleberries into a basin of water; take off, whatever floats; take up the berries by the handful, pick out all the stems and unripe berries and put them into a dish; line a buttered pie, dish with a pie paste, put in the berries half an inch deep, and to a quart of berries, put half of a teacupful of brown sugar; dredge a teaspoonful of flour over, strew a saltspoonful of salt and a little nutmeg grated over; cover the pie, cut a slit in the centre, or make several small incisions on either side of it; press the two crusts together around the edge, trim it off neatly with a sharp knife and bake in a quick oven for three-quarters of an hour.

BLACKBERRY PIE.

Pick the berries clean, rinse them in cold water and finish as directed for huckleberries.

MOLASSES PIE.

Two teacupfuls of molasses; one of sugar, three eggs, one tablespoonful of melted butter, one lemon, nutmeg; beat and bake in pastry.

LEMON RAISIN PIE.

One cup of chopped raisins, seeded, and the juice and grated rind of one lemon, one cupful of cold water, one tablespoonful of flour, one cupful of sugar, two tablespoonfuls of butter. Stir lightly together and bake with upper and under crust.

RHUBARB PIE.

Cut the large stalks off where the leaves commence, strip off the outside skin, then cut the stalks in pieces half an inch long; line a pie dish with paste rolled rather thicker than a dollar piece, put a layer of the rhubarb nearly an inch deep; to a quart bowl of cut rhubarb put a large teacupful of sugar; strew it over with a saltspoonful of salt and a little nutmeg grated; shake over a little flour; cover with a rich pie crust, cut a slit in the centre, trim off the edge with a sharp knife and bake in a quick oven until the pie loosens from the dish. Rhubarb pies made in this way are altogether superior to those made of the fruit stewed.

RHUBARB PIE. (Cooked.)

Skin the stalks, cut them into small pieces, wash and put them in a stewpan with no more water than what adheres to them; when cooked, mash them fine and put in a small piece of butter; when cool, sweeten to taste; if liked, add a little lemon-peel, cinnamon or nutmeg; line your plate with thin crust, put in the filling, cover with crust and bake in a *quick* oven; sift sugar over it when served.

PINEAPPLE PIE.

A grated pineapple, its weight in sugar, half its weight in butter, one cupful of cream, five eggs; beat the batter to a creamy froth, add the sugar and yolks of the eggs, continue beating till very light; add the cream, the pineapple grated and the whites of the eggs beaten to a stiff froth. Bake with an under crust. Eat cold.

GRAPE PIE.

Pop the pulps out of the skins into one dish and put the skins into another. Then simmer the pulp a little over the fire to soften it; remove it and rub it through a colander to separate it from the seeds. Then put the skins and pulp together and they are ready for pies or for canning or putting in jugs for other use. Fine for pies.

DAMSON OR PLUM PIE.

Stew the damsons whole in water only sufficient to prevent their burning; when tender and while hot, sweeten them with sugar and let them stand until they become cold; then pour them into pie dishes lined with paste, dredge flour upon them, cover them with the same paste, wet and pinch together the edges of the paste, cut a slit in the centre of the cover through which the vapor may escape and bake twenty minutes.

CHOPPING THE MINCEMEAT.

PEACH PIE.

Peel, stone and slice the peaches. Line a pie plate with crust and lay in your fruit, sprinkling sugar liberally over them in proportion to their sweetness. Allow three peach kernels chopped fine to each pie; pour in a very little water and bake with an upper crust, or with cross-bars of paste across the top.

DRIED FRUIT PIES.

Wash the fruit thoroughly, soak over night in water enough to cover. In the morning stew slowly until nearly done in the same water. Sweeten to taste. The crust, both upper and under, should be rolled thin; a thick crust to a fruit pie is undesirable.

RIPE BERRY PIES.

All made the same as "Cherry Pie." Line your pie-tin with crust, fill half full of berries, shake over a tablespoonful of sifted flour (if very juicy) and as much sugar as is necessary to sweeten sufficiently. Now fill up the crust to the top, making quite full. Cover with crust and bake about forty minutes.

Huckleberry and blackberry pies are improved by putting into them a little ginger and cinnamon.

JELLY AND PRESERVED FRUIT PIES.

Preserved fruit requires no baking; hence, always bake the shell and put in the sweetmeats afterwards; you can cover with whipped cream, or bake a top crust shell; the former is preferable for delicacy.

CRANBERRY PIE.

Take fine, sound, ripe cranberries and with a sharp knife split each one until you have a heaping coffeecupful; put them in a vegetable dish or basin; put over them one cupful of white sugar, half a cup of water, a tablespoon *full* of sifted flour; stir it all together and put into your crust. Cover with an upper crust and bake slowly in a moderate oven. You will find this the true way of making a cranberry pie.

CRANBERRY TART PIE.

After having washed and picked over the berries, stew them well in a little water, just enough to cover them; when they burst open and become soft, sweeten them with plenty of sugar, mash them smooth (some prefer them not mashed); line your pie-plates with thin puff paste, fill them and lay strips of paste across the top. Bake in a moderate oven. Or you may rub them through a colander to free them from the skins.

GOOSEBERRY PIE.

Can be made the same as "Cranberry Tart Pie," or an upper crust can be put on before baking. Serve with boiled custard or a pitcher of good sweet cream.

STEWED PUMPKIN OR SQUASH FOR PIES.

Deep-colored pumpkins are generally the best. Cut a pumpkin or squash in half, take out the seeds, then cut it up in thick slices, pare the outside and cut again in small pieces. Put it into a large pot or saucepan with a very little water; let it cook slowly until tender. Now set the pot on the back of the stove, where it will not burn, and cook slowly, stirring often until the moisture is dried out and the pumpkin looks dark and red. It requires cooking a long time, at least half a day, to have it dry and rich. When cool press through a colander.

BAKED PUMPKIN OR SQUASH FOR PIES.

Cut up in several pieces, do not pare it; place them on baking tins and set them in the oven; bake slowly until soft, then take them out, scrape all the pumpkin from the shell, rub it through a colander. It will be fine and light and free from lumps.

PUMPKIN PIE. No. 1.

For three pies: One quart of milk, three cupfuls of boiled and strained pumpkin, one and one-half cupfuls of sugar, one-half cupful of molasses, the yolks and whites of four eggs beaten separately, a little salt, one tablespoonful each of ginger and cinnamon. Beat all together and bake with an under crust.

Boston marrow or Hubbard squash may be substituted for pumpkin and are much preferred by many, as possessing a less strong flavor.

PUMPKIN PIE. No. 2.

One quart of stewed pumpkin pressed through a sieve, nine eggs, whites and yolks beaten separately, two scant quarts of milk, one teaspoonful of mace, one teaspoonful of cinnamon and the same of nutmeg, one and one-half cupfuls of white sugar, or very light brown. Beat all well together and bake in crust without cover.

A tablespoonful of brandy is a great improvement to pumpkin, or squash pies.

PUMPKIN PIE WITHOUT EGGS.

One quart of properly stewed pumpkin pressed through a colander; to this add enough good, rich milk, sufficient to moisten it enough to fill two good-sized earthen pie-plates, a teaspoonful of salt, half a cupful of molasses or brown sugar, a tablespoonful of ginger, one teaspoonful of cinnamon or nutmeg. Bake in a moderately slow oven three-quarters of an hour.

SQUASH PIE.

One pint of boiled dry squash, one cupful of brown sugar, three eggs, two tablespoonfuls of molasses, one tablespoonful of melted butter one tablespoonful of ginger, one teaspoonful of cinnamon, a pinch of salt and one pint of milk. This makes two pies, or one large deep one.

SWEET POTATO PIE.

One pound of steamed sweet potatoes finely mashed,-two cups sugar, one cup cream, one-half cup butter, three well-beaten eggs, flavor with lemon or nutmeg and bake in pastry shell. Fine.

COOKED MEAT FOR MINCE PIES.

In order to succeed in having good mince pie, it is quite essential to cook the meat properly, so as to retain its juices and strength of flavor.

Select four pounds of lean beef, the neck piece is as good as any; wash it and put it into a kettle with just water enough to cover it; take off the scum as it reaches the boiling point, add hot water from time to time, until it is tender, then season with salt and pepper; take off the cover and let it boil until almost dry, or until the juice has boiled back into the meat. When it looks as though it was beginning to fry in its own juice, it is time to take up and set aside to get cold, which should be done the day before needed. Next day, when making the mince meat, the bones, gristle and stringy bits should be well picked out before chopping.

MINCE PIES. No. 1.

The "Astor House," some years ago, was *famous* for its "mince pies." The chief pastry cook at that time, by request, published the recipe. I find that those who partake of it never fail to speak in laudable terms of the superior excellence of this recipe when strictly followed.

Four pounds of lean boiled beef chopped fine, twice as much of chopped green tart apples, one pound of chopped suet, three pounds of raisins, seeded, two pounds of currants picked over, washed and dried, half a pound of citron, cut up fine, one pound of brown sugar, one quart of cooking molasses, two quarts of sweet cider, one pint of boiled cider, one tablespoonful of salt, one tablespoonful of pepper, one tablespoonful of mace, one tablespoonful of allspice and four tablespoonfuls of cinnamon, two grated nutmegs, one tablespoonful of cloves; mix thoroughly and warm it on the range until heated through. Remove from the fire and when nearly cool, stir in a pint of good brandy and one pint of Madeira wine. Put into a crock, cover it tightly and set it in a cold place where it will not freeze, but keep perfectly cold. Will keep good all winter.

MINCE PIES. No. 2.

Two pounds of lean fresh beef, boiled and, when cold, chopped fine. One pound of beef suet, cleared of strings and minced to powder. Five pounds of apples, pared and chopped, two pounds of raisins, seeded and chopped, one pound of Sultana raisins, washed and picked over, two pounds of currants washed and *carefully* picked over, three-quarters of a pound of citron cut up fine, two tablespoonfuls cinnamon, one of powdered nutmeg, two of mace, one of cloves, one of allspice, one of fine salt, two and a quarter pounds of brown sugar, one quart brown sherry, one pint best brandy.

Mince-meat made by this recipe will keep all winter. Cover closely in a jar and set in a cool place.

For preserving mince meat, look for CANNED MINCE MEAT.

MOCK MINCE MEAT WITHOUT MEAT.

One cupful of cold water, half a cupful of molasses, half a cupful of brown sugar, half a cupful of cider vinegar, two-thirds of a cupful of melted butter, one cupful of raisins seeded and chopped, one egg beaten light, half a cupful of rolled cracker crumbs, a teaspoonful of cinnamon, a teaspoonful each of cloves, allspice, nutmeg, salt and black pepper.

Put the saucepan on the fire with the water and raisins; let them cook a few minutes, then add the sugar and molasses, then the vinegar, then the other ingredients; lastly, add a wine-glassful of brandy. Very fine.

FRUIT TURNOVERS. (Suitable for Picnics.)

Make a nice puff paste; roll it out the usual thickness, as for pies; then cut it out into circular pieces about the size of a small tea saucer; pile the fruit on half of the paste, sprinkle over some sugar, wet the edges and turn the paste over. Press the edges together, ornament them and brush the turnovers over with the white of an egg; sprinkle over sifted sugar and bake on tins, in a brisk oven, for about twenty minutes. Instead of putting the fruit in raw, it may be boiled down with a little sugar first and then enclosed in the crust; or jam of any kind may be substituted for fresh fruit.

PLUM CUSTARD TARTLETS.

One pint of greengage plums, after being rubbed through a sieve, one large cup of sugar, the yolks of two eggs well beaten. Whisk all together until light and foamy, then bake in small patty-pans shells of puff paste a light brown. Then fill with the plum paste, beat the two whites until stiff, add two tablespoonfuls of powdered sugar, spread over the plum paste and set the shells into a moderate oven for a few moments.

These are much more easily handled than pieces of pie or even pies whole, and can be packed nicely for carrying.

LEMON TARTLETS. No. 1.

Put a quart of milk into a saucepan over the fire. When it comes to the boiling point put into it the following mixture: Into a bowl put a heaping tablespoonful of flour, half a cupful of sugar and a pinch of salt. Stir this all together thoroughly; then add the beaten yolks of six eggs; stir this one way into the boiling milk until cooked to a thick cream; remove from the fire and stir into it the grated rind and juice of one large lemon. Have ready baked and hot some puff paste tart shells. Fill them with the custard and cover each with a meringue made of the whites of the eggs, sweetened with four tablespoonfuls of sugar. Put into the oven and bake a light straw color.

LEMON TARTLETS. No. 2.

Mix well together the juice and grated rind of two lemons, two cupfuls of sugar, two eggs and the crumbs of sponge cake; beat it all together until smooth; put into twelve patty-pans lined with puff paste and bake until the crust is done.

ORANGE TARTLETS.

Take the juice of two large oranges and the grated peel of one, three-fourths of a cup of sugar, a tablespoonful of butter; stir in a good teaspoonful of cornstarch into the juice of half a lemon and add to the mixture. Beat all well together and bake in tart shells without cover.

MERINGUE CUSTARD TARTLETS.

Select deep individual pie-tins; fluted tartlet pans are suitable for custard tarts, but they should be about six inches in diameter and from two to three inches deep. Butter the pan and line it with ordinary puff paste, then fill it with a custard made as follows: Stir gradually into the beaten yolks of six eggs two tablespoonfuls of flour, a saltspoonful of salt and half a pint of cream. Stir until free from lumps and add two tablespoonfuls of sugar; put the saucepan on the range and stir until the custard coats the spoon. Do not let it boil or it will curdle. Pour it in a bowl, add a few drops of vanilla flavoring and stir until the custard becomes cold; fill the lined mold with this and bake in a moderate oven. In the meantime, put the whites of the eggs in a bright copper vessel and beat thoroughly, using a baker's wire egg-beater for this purpose. While beating, sprinkle in lightly half a pound of sugar and a dash of salt. When the paste is quite firm, spread a thin layer of it over the tart and decorate the top with the remainder by squeezing it through a paper funnel. Strew a little powdered sugar over the top, return to the oven, and when a delicate yellow tinge remove from the oven and when cold serve.

BERRY TARTS.

Line small pie-tins with pie crust and bake. Just before ready to use fill the tarts with strawberries, blackberries, raspberries, or whatever berries are in season. Sprinkle over each tart a little sugar; after adding berries add also to each tart a tablespoonful of sweet cream. They form a delicious addition to the breakfast table.

CREAM STRAWBERRY TARTS.

After picking over the berries carefully, arrange them in layers in a deep pie-tin lined with puff paste, sprinkling sugar thickly between each layer: fill the pie-tin pretty full, pouring in a quantity of the juice: cover with a thick crust, with a slit in the top and bake. When the pie is baked, pour into the slit in the top of the pie the following cream mixture: Take a small cupful of the cream from the top of the morning's milk, heat it until it comes to a boil, then stir into it the whites of two eggs beaten light, also a tablespoonful of white sugar and a teaspoonful of cornstarch wet in cold milk. Boil all together a few moments until quite smooth; set it aside and when cool pour it into the pie through the slit in the crust. Serve it cold with powdered sugar sifted over it.

Raspberry, blackberry and whortleberry may be made the same.

GREEN GOOSEBERRY TART.

Top and tail the gooseberries. Put into a porcelain kettle with enough water to prevent burning and stew slowly until they break. Take them off, sweeten *well* and set aside to cool. When cold pour into pastry shells and bake with a top crust of puff paste. Brush all over with beaten egg while hot, set back in the oven to glaze for three minutes. Eat cold.

COCOANUT TARTS.

Take three cocoanuts, the meats grated, the yolks of five eggs, half a cupful of white sugar, season, a wine-glass of milk; put the butter in cold and bake in a nice puff paste.

CHOCOLATE TARTS.

Four eggs, whites and yolks, one-half cake of Baker's chocolate, grated, one tablespoonful of cornstarch, dissolved in water, three tablespoonfuls of milk, four of white sugar, two teaspoonfuls of vanilla, one saltspoonful of salt, one-half teaspoonful of cinnamon, one teaspoonful of butter, melted; rub the chocolate smooth in the milk and heat to boiling over the fire, then stir in the cornstarch. Stir five minutes until well thickened, remove from the fire and pour into a bowl. Beat all the yolks and the whites of two eggs well with the sugar, and when the chocolate mixture is almost cold, put all together with the flavoring and stir until light. Bake in open shells of pastry. When done, cover with a meringue made of the whites of two eggs and two tablespoonfuls of sugar flavored with a teaspoonful of lemon juice. Eat cold.

These are nice for tea, baked in patty-pans.

MAIDS OF HONOR.

Take one cupful of sour milk, one of sweet milk, a tablespoonful of melted butter, the yolks of four eggs, juice and rind of one lemon and a small cupful of white pounded sugar. Put both kinds of milk together in a vessel, which is set in another and let it become sufficiently heated to set the curd, then strain off the milk, rub the curd through a strainer, add butter to the curd, the sugar, well-beaten eggs and lemon. Line the little pans with the richest of puff paste and fill with the mixture; bake until firm in the centre, from ten to fifteen minutes.

GERMAN FRUIT PIE.

Sift together a heaping teaspoonful of baking powder and a pint of flour; add a piece of butter as large as a walnut, a pinch of salt, one beaten egg and sweet milk enough to make a soft dough. Roll it out half an inch thick; butter a square biscuit tin and cover the bottom and sides with the dough; fill the pan with quartered juicy apples, sprinkle with a little cinnamon and molasses. Bake in rather quick oven until the crust and apples are cooked a light brown. Sprinkle a little sugar over the top five minutes before removing from the oven.

Ripe peaches are fine used in the same manner.

APPLE TARTS.

Pare, quarter, core and boil in half a cupful of water, until quite soft, ten large, tart apples; beat until very smooth and add the yolks of six eggs, or three whole ones, the juice and grated outside rind of two lemons, half a cap of butter; one and a half of sugar (or more, if not sufficiently sweet); beat all thoroughly, line patty-pans with a puff paste and fill; bake five minutes in a hot oven.

Meringue.—If desired very nice, cover them when removed from the oven with the meringue made of the whites of three eggs remaining, mixed with three tablespoonfuls of sugar; return to the oven and delicately brown.

CREAM TARTS.

Make a rich, brittle crust, with which cover your patty-pans, smoothing off the edges nicely and bake well. While these "shells" are cooling, take one teacupful (more or less according to the number of tarts you want) of perfectly sweet and fresh cream, skimmed free of milk; put this into a large bowl or other deep dish, and with your egg-beater whip it to a thick, stiff froth; add a heaping tablespoonful of fine white sugar, with a teaspoonful (a small one) of lemon or vanilla. Fill the cold shells with this and set in a cool place till tea is ready.

OPEN JAM TARTS.

Time to bake until paste loosens from the dish. Line shallow tin dish with puff paste, put in the jam, roll out some of the paste, wet it lightly with the yolk of an egg beaten with a little milk, and a tablespoonful of powdered sugar. Cut it in narrow strips, then lay them across the tart, lay another strip around the edge, trim off outside, and bake in a quick oven.

CHESS CAKES.

Peel and grate one cocoanut; boil one pound of sugar fifteen minutes in two-thirds of a pint of water; stir in the grated cocoanut and boil fifteen minutes longer. While warm, stir in a quarter of a pound of butter; add the yolks of seven eggs well beaten. Bake in patty-pans with rich paste. If prepared cocoanut is used, take one and a half coffeecupfuls. Fine.

CUSTARDS, CREAMS AND DESSERTS.

The usual rule for custards is, eight eggs to a quart of milk; but a very good custard can be made of six, or even less, especially with the addition of a level tablespoonful of sifted flour, thoroughly blended in the sugar first, before adding the other ingredients. They may be baked, boiled or steamed, either in cups or one large dish. It improves custard to first boil the milk and then cool it before being used; also a little salt adds to the flavor. A very small lump of butter may also be added, if one wants something especially rich.

To make custards look and taste better, duck's eggs should be used when obtainable; they add very much to the flavor and richness, and so many are not required as of ordinary eggs, four duck's eggs to the pint of milk making a delicious custard. When desired extremely rich and good, cream should be substituted for the milk, and double the quantity of eggs used to those mentioned, omitting the whites.

When making boiled custard, set the dish containing the custard into another and larger dish, partly filled with boiling water, placed over the fire. Let the cream or milk come almost to a boil before adding the eggs or thickening, then stir it briskly one way every moment until smooth and well cooked; it must *not* boil or it will curdle.

To bake a custard, the fire should be moderate and the dish well buttered.

Everything in baked custard depends upon the *regularly heated slow* oven. If made with nicety it is the most delicate of all sweets; if cooked till it wheys it is hardly eatable.

Frozen eggs can be made quite as good as fresh ones if used as soon as thawed soft. Drop them into boiling water, letting them remain until the water is cold. They will be soft all through and beat up equal to those that have not been touched with the frost.

Eggs should always be thoroughly well beaten separately, the yolks first, then the sugar added, beat again, then add the beaten whites with the flavoring, then the cooled scalded milk. The lighter the eggs are beaten, the thicker and richer the custard.

Eggs should always be broken into a cup, the whites and yolks separated, and they should always be strained. Breaking the eggs thus, the bad ones may be easily rejected without spoiling the others and so cause no waste.

A meringue, or frosting for the top, requires about a tablespoonful of fine sugar to the beaten white of one egg; to be placed on the top after the custard or pudding is baked, smoothed over with a broad-bladed knife dipped in cold water, and replaced in the oven to brown slightly.

SOFT CARAMEL CUSTARD.

One quart of milk, half a cupful of sugar, six eggs, half a teaspoonful of salt. Put the milk on to boil, reserving a cupful. Beat the eggs and add the cold milk to them. Stir the sugar in a small frying pan until it becomes liquid and just begins to smoke. Stir it into the boiling milk; then add the beaten eggs and cold milk and stir constantly until the mixture begins to thicken. Set away to cool. Serve in glasses.

BAKED CUSTARD.

Beat five fresh eggs, the whites and yolks separately, the yolks with half a cup of sugar, the whites to a stiff froth; then stir them gradually into a quart of sweet rich milk previously boiled and cooled; flavor with extract of lemon or vanilla and half a teaspoonful of salt. Rub butter over the bottom and sides of a baking-dish or tin basin; pour in the custard, grate a little nutmeg over and bake in a quick oven. It is better to set the dish in a shallow pan of hot water reaching nearly to the top, the water to be kept boiling until the custard is baked; three-quarters of an hour is generally enough. Run a teaspoon handle into the middle of it; if it comes out clean it is baked sufficiently.

CUP CUSTARD.

Six eggs half a cupful of sugar, one quart of new milk. Beat the eggs and the sugar and milk, and any extract or flavoring you like. Fill your custard cups, sift a little nutmeg or cinnamon over the tops, set them in a moderate oven in a shallow pan half filled with hot water. In about twenty minutes try them with the handle of a teaspoon to see if they are firm. Judgment and great care are needed to attain skill in baking custard, for if left in the oven a minute too long, or if the fire is too hot, the milk will certainly whey.

Serve cold with fresh fruit sugared and placed on top of each. Strawberries, peaches or raspberries, as preferred.

BOILED CUSTARD.

Beat seven eggs very light, omitting the whites of two; mix them gradually with a quart of milk and half a cupful of sugar; boil in a dish set in another of boiling water; add flavoring. As soon as it comes to the boiling point remove it, or it will be liable to curdle and become lumpy. Whip the whites of the two eggs that remain, adding two heaping tablespoonfuls of sugar. When the custard is cold heap this on top; if in cups, put on a strawberry or a bit of red jelly on each. Set in a cold place till wanted.

BOILED CUSTARD, OR MOCK CREAM.

Take two even tablespoonfuls of cornstarch, one quart of milk, three eggs, half a teaspoonful of salt and a small piece of butter; heat the milk to nearly boiling and add the starch, previously dissolved in a little cold milk; then add the eggs well beaten with four tablespoonfuls of powdered sugar; let it boil up once or twice, stirring it briskly, and it is done. Flavor with lemon, or vanilla, or raspberry, or to suit your taste.

A good substitute for ice cream, served *very* cold.

FRENCH CUSTARD.

One quart of milk, eight eggs, sugar and cinnamon to taste; separate the eggs, beat the yolks until thick, to which add the milk, a little vanilla, and sweeten to taste; put it into a pan or farina kettle, place it over a slow fire and stir it all the time until it becomes custard; then pour it into a pudding-dish to get cold; whisk the whites until stiff and dry; have ready a pan of boiling water on the top of which place the whites; cover and place them where the water will keep sufficiently hot to cause a steam to pass through and cook them; place in a dish (suitable for the table) a layer of custard and white alternately; on each layer of custard grate a little nutmeg with a teaspoonful of wine; reserve a layer of white for the cover, over which grate nutmeg; then send to table and eat cold.

GERMAN CUSTARD.

Add to a pint of good, rich, boiled custard an ounce of sweet almonds, blanched, roasted and pounded to a paste, and half an ounce of pine-nuts or peanuts, blanched, roasted and pounded; also a small quantity of candied citron cut into the thinnest possible slips; cook the custard as usual and set it on the ice for some hours before using.

APPLE CUSTARD.

Pare, core and quarter a dozen large juicy pippins. Stew among them the yellow peel of a large lemon grated very fine, and stew them till tender in a very small portion of water. When done, mash them smooth with the back of a spoon (you must have a pint and a half of the stewed apple); mix a half cupful of sugar with them and set them away till cold. Beat six eggs very light and stir them gradually into a quart of rich milk alternately with the stewed apple. Put the mixture into cups, or into a deep dish and bake it about twenty minutes. Send it to table cold, with nutmeg grated over the top.

ALMOND CUSTARD. No. 1.

Scald and blanch half a pound of shelled sweet almonds and three ounces of bitter almonds, throwing them, as you do them, into a large bowl of cold water. Then pound them one at a time into a paste, adding a few drops of wine or rose-water to them. Beat eight eggs very light with two-thirds of a cup of sugar, then mix together with a quart of rich milk, or part milk and part cream; put the mixture into a saucepan and set it over the fire. Stir it one way until it begins to thicken, but not till it curdles; remove from the fire and when it is cooled put in a glass dish. Having reserved part of the whites of the eggs, beat them to a stiff froth, season with three tablespoonfuls of sugar and a teaspoonful of lemon extract, spread over the top of the custard. Serve cold.

ALMOND CUSTARD. No. 2.

Blanch a quarter of a pound of sweet almonds, pound them, as in No. 1 on preceding page, with six ounces of fine white sugar and mix them well with the yolks of four eggs; then dissolve one ounce of patent gelatine in one quart of boiling milk, strain it through a sieve and pour into it the other mixture; stir the whole over the fire until it thickens and is smooth; then pour it into your mold and keep it upon ice, or in a cool place, until wanted; when ready to serve dip the mold into warm water, rub it with a cloth and turn out the cream carefully upon your dish.

SNOWBALL CUSTARD.

Soak half a package of Cox's gelatine in a teacupful of cold water one hour, to which add a pint of boiling water, stir it until the gelatine is thoroughly dissolved. Then beat the whites of four eggs to a stiff froth, put two teacupfuls of sugar in the gelatine water first, then the beaten white of egg and one teaspoonful of vanilla extract, or the grated rind and the juice of a lemon. Whip it some time until it is all quite stiff and cold. Dip some teacups or wine-glasses in cold water and fill them; set in a cold place.

In the meantime, make a boiled custard of the yolks of three of the eggs, with half a cupful of sugar and a pint of milk; flavor with vanilla extract. Now after the meringue in the cups has stood four or five hours, turn them out of the molds, place them in a glass dish and pour this custard around the base.

BAKED COCOANUT CUSTARD.

Grate as much cocoanut as will weigh a pound. Mix half a pound of powdered white sugar with the milk of the cocoanut, or with a pint of cream, adding two tablespoonfuls of rose-water. Then stir in gradually a pint of rich milk. Beat to a stiff froth the whites of eight eggs and stir them into the milk and sugar, a little at a time, alternately with the grated cocoanut; add a teaspoonful of powdered nutmeg and cinnamon. Then put the mixture into cups and bake them twenty minutes in a moderate oven, set in a pan half filled with boiling water. When cold, grate loaf sugar over them.

WHIPPED CREAM. No. 1.

To the whites of three eggs, beaten to a stiff froth, add a pint of thick sweet cream (previously set where it is very cold) and four tablespoonfuls of sweet wine, with three of fine white sugar and a teaspoonful of the extract of lemon or vanilla. Mix all the ingredients together on a board platter or pan and whip it to a standing froth; as the froth rises, take it off lightly with a spoon and lay it on an inverted sieve with a dish under it to catch what will drain through; and what drains through can be beaten over again.

Serve in a glass dish with jelly or jam and sliced sponge cake. This should be whipped in a cool place and set in the ice box.

WHIPPED CREAM. No. 2.

Three coffeecupfuls of good thick sweet cream, half a cup of powdered sugar, three teaspoonfuls of vanilla; whip it to a stiff froth. Dissolve three-fourths of an ounce of best gelatine in a teacup of hot water and when cool pour it in the cream and stir it gently from the bottom upward, cutting the cream into it, until it thickens. The dish which contains the cream should be set in another dish containing ice-water, or cracked ice. When finished pour in molds and set on ice or in any very cold place.

SPANISH CREAM.

Take one quart of milk and soak half a box of gelatine in it for an hour; place it on the fire and stir often. Beat the yolks of three eggs very light with a cupful of sugar, stir into the scalding milk and heat until it begins to thicken (it should not boil, or it will curdle); remove from the fire and strain through thin muslin or tarlatan, and when nearly cold flavor with vanilla or lemon; then wet a dish or mold in cold water and set aside to stiffen.

BAVARIAN CREAM.

One quart of sweet cream, the yolks of four eggs beaten together with a cupful of sugar. Dissolve half an ounce of gelatine or isinglass in half a teacupful of warm water; when it is dissolved stir in a pint of boiling hot cream; add the beaten yolks and sugar; cook all together until it begins to thicken, then remove from the fire and add the other pint of cold cream whipped to a stiff froth, adding a little at a time and beating hard. Season with vanilla or lemon. Whip the whites of the eggs for the top. Dip the mold in cold water before filling; set it in a cold place. To this could be added almonds, pounded, grated chocolate, peaches, pineapples, strawberries, raspberries, or any seasonable fruit.

STRAWBERRY BAVARIAN CREAM.

Pick off the hulls of a box of strawberries, bruise them in a basin with a cup of powered sugar; rub this through a sieve and mix with it a pint of whipped cream and one ounce and a half of clarified isinglass or gelatine; pour the cream into a mold previously oiled. Let it in rough ice and when it has become firm turn out on a dish.

Raspberries or currants may be substituted for strawberries.

GOLDEN CREAM.

Boil a quart of milk; when boiling stir into it the well-beaten yolks of six eggs; add six tablespoonfuls of sugar and one tablespoonful of sifted flour, which have been well beaten together; when boiled, turn it into a dish, and pour over it the whites beaten to a stiff froth, mixing with them six tablespoonfuls, of powdered sugar. Set all in the oven and brown slightly. Flavor the top with vanilla and the bottom with lemon. Serve cold.

CHOCOLATE CREAM. No. 1.

Three ounces of grated chocolate, one-quarter pound of sugar, one and one-half pints of cream, one and one-half ounces of clarified isinglass, or gelatine, the yolks of six eggs.

Beat the yolks of the eggs well; put them into a basin with the grated chocolate, the sugar and one pint of the cream; stir these ingredients well together, pour them into a basin and set this basin in a saucepan of boiling water; stir it one way until the mixture thickens, but *do not allow it to boil*, or it will curdle. Strain the cream through a sieve into a basin, stir in the isinglass and the other one-half pint of cream, which should-be well whipped; mix all well together, and pour it into a mold which has been previously oiled with the purest salad oil, and, if at hand, set it in ice until wanted for table.

CHOCOLATE CREAM OR CUSTARD. No. 2.

Take one quart of milk, and when nearly boiling stir in two ounces of grated chocolate; let it warm on the fire for a few moments, and then remove and cool; beat the yolks of eight eggs and two whites with eight tablespoonfuls of sugar, then pour the milk over them; flavor and bake as any custard, either in cups or a large dish. Make a meringue of the remaining whites.

LEMON CREAM. No. 1.

One pint of cream, the yolks of two eggs, one quarter of a pound of white sugar, one large lemon, one ounce isinglass or gelatine.

Put the cream into a *lined* saucepan with the sugar, lemon peel and isinglass, and simmer these over a gentle fire for about ten minutes, stirring them all the time. Strain the cream into a basin, add the yolks of eggs, which should be well beaten, and put the basin into a saucepan of boiling water; stir the mixture one way until it thickens, *but do not allow it to boil*; take it off the fire and keep stirring it until nearly cold. Strain the lemon juice into a basin, gradually pour on it the cream, and *stir it well* until the juice is well mixed with it. Have ready a well-oiled mold, pour the cream into it, and let it remain until perfectly set. When required for table, loosen the edges with a small blunt knife, put a dish on the top of the mold, turn it over quickly, and the cream should easily slip away.

LEMON CREAM. No. 2.

Pare into one quart of boiling water the peels of four large lemons, the yellow outside only; let it stand for four hours;

then take them out and add to the water the juice of the four lemons and one cupful of fine white sugar. Beat the yolks of ten eggs and mix all together; strain it through a piece of lawn or lace into a porcelain lined stewpan; set it over a slow fire; stir it one way until it is as thick as good cream, *but do not let it boil*; then take it from the fire, and, when cool, serve in custard cups.

LEMON CREAM. No. 3.

Peel three lemons and squeeze out the juice into one quart of milk. Add the peel; cut in pieces and cover the mixture for a few hours; then add six eggs, well beaten, and one pint of water, well sweetened. Strain and simmer over a gentle fire till it thickens; *do not let it boil.* Serve very cold.

ORANGE CREAM.

Whip a pint of cream so long that there will be but one-half the quantity left when skimmed off. Soak in half a cupful of cold water a half package of gelatine and then grate over it the rind of two oranges. Strain the juice of six oranges and add to it a cupful of sugar; now put the half pint of unwhipped cream into a double boiler, pour into it the well-beaten yolks of six eggs, stirring until it begins to thicken, then add the gelatine. Remove from the fire, let it stand for two minutes and add the orange juice and sugar; beat all together until about the consistency of soft custard and add the whipped cream. Mix well and turn into molds to harden. To be served with sweetened cream. Fine.

SOLID CREAM.

Four tablespoonfuls of pounded sugar, one quart of cream, two tablespoonfuls of brandy, the juice of one large lemon.

Strain the lemon juice over the sugar and add the brandy, then stir in the cream, put the mixture into a pitcher and continue pouring from one pitcher to another, until it is quite thick; or it may be whisked until the desired consistency is obtained. It should be served in jelly glasses.

BANANA CREAM.

After peeling the bananas, mash them with an iron or wooden spoon; allow equal quantities of bananas and sweet cream; to one quart of the mixture, allow one-quarter of a pound of sugar. Beat them all together until the cream is light.

TAPIOCA CREAM CUSTARD.

Soak three heaping tablespoonfuls of tapioca in a teacupful of water over night. Place over the fire a quart of milk; let it come to a boil, then stir in the tapioca, a good pinch of salt, stir until it thickens; then add a cupful of sugar and the beaten yolks of three eggs. Stir it quickly and pour it into a dish and stir gently into the mixture the whites beaten stiff, the flavoring and set it on ice, or in an ice chest.

PEACH CREAM. No. 1.

Mash very smooth two cupfuls of canned peaches, run them through a sieve and cook for three minutes in a syrup made by boiling together one cupful of sugar and stirring all the time. Place the pan containing the syrup and peaches into another of boiling water and add one-half packet of gelatine prepared the same as in previous recipes, and stir for five minutes to thoroughly dissolve the gelatine, then take it from the fire, place in a pan of ice-water, beat until nearly cool and then add the well-frothed whites of six eggs. Beat this whole mixture until it commences to harden. Then pour into a mold, set away to cool and serve with cream and sugar. It should be placed on the ice to cool for two or three hours before serving.

PEACH CREAM. No. 2.

A quart of fine peaches, pare and stone the fruit and cut in quarters. Beat the whites of three eggs with a half cupful of powdered sugar until it is stiff enough to cut with a knife. Take the yolks and mix with half a cupful of granulated sugar and a pint of milk. Put the peaches into the mixture, place in a pudding-dish and bake until almost firm; then put in the whites, mixing all thoroughly again, and bake a light brown. Eat ice cold.

ITALIAN CREAM.

Put two pints of cream into two bowls; with one bowl mix six ounces of powdered loaf sugar, the juice of two large lemons and two glassfuls of white wine; then add the other pint of cream and stir the whole very hard; boil two ounces of isinglass or gelatine with four small teacupfuls of water till reduced to one-half; then stir the mixture luke-warm into the other ingredients; put them in a glass dish to congeal.

SNOW CREAM.

Heat a quart of thick, sweet cream; when ready to boil, stir into it quickly three tablespoonfuls of cornstarch flour, blended with some cold cream; sweeten to taste and allow it to boil gently, stirring for two or three minutes; add quickly the whites of six eggs, beaten to a stiff froth; do not allow it to boil up more than once after adding the eggs; flavor with lemon, vanilla, bitter almond or grated lemon peel; lay the snow thus formed quickly in rocky heaps on silver or glass dishes, or in shapes. Iced, it will turn out well.

If the recipe is closely followed, any family may enjoy it at a trifling expense, and it is really worthy the table of an epicure. It can be made the day before it is to be eaten; kept cold.

MOCK ICE.

Take about three tablespoonfuls of some good preserve; rub it through a sieve with as much cream as will fill a quart mold; dissolve three-quarters of an ounce of isinglass or gelatine in half a pint of water; when almost cold, mix it well with the cream; put it into a mold, set in a cool place and turn out next day.

PEACH MERINGUE.

Pare and quarter (removing stones) a quart of sound, ripe peaches; place them all in a dish that it will not injure to set in the oven and yet be suitable to place on the table. Sprinkle the peaches with sugar, and cover them well with the beaten whites of three eggs. Stand the dish in the oven until the eggs have become a delicate brown, then remove, and when cool enough, set the dish on ice, or in a very cool place. Take the yolks of the eggs, add to them a pint of milk, sweeten and flavor, and boil same in a custard kettle, being careful to keep the eggs from curdling. When cool pour into a glass pitcher and serve with the meringue when ready to use.

APPLE FLOAT.

One dozen apples, pared and cored, one pound and a half of sugar. Put the apples on with water enough to cover them and let them stew until they look as if they would break; then take them out and put the sugar in the same water; let the syrup come to a boil, put in the apples and let them stew until done through and clear; then take them out, slice into the syrup one large lemon and add an ounce of gelatine dissolved in a pint of cold water. Let the whole mix well and come to a boil; then pour upon the apples. The syrup will congeal. It is to be eaten cold with cream.

Or you may change the dish by making a soft custard with the yolks of four eggs, three tablespoonfuls of powdered sugar and a scant quart of milk. When cold, spread it over the apples. Whip the whites of the egg, flavor with lemon and place on the custard. Color in the oven.

SYLLABUB.

One quart of rich milk or cream, a cupful of wine, half a cupful of sugar; put the sugar and wine into a bowl and the milk lukewarm in a separate vessel. When the sugar is dissolved in the wine, pour the milk in, holding it high; pour it back and forth until it is frothy. Grate nutmeg over it.

CREAM FOR FRUIT.

This recipe is an excellent substitute for pure cream, to be eaten on fresh berries and fruit.

One cupful of sweet milk; heat it until boiling. Beat together the whites of two eggs, a tablespoonful of white sugar and a piece of butter the size of a nutmeg. Now add half a cupful of cold milk and a teaspoonful of cornstarch; stir well together until very light and smooth, then add it to the boiling milk; cook it until it thickens; it must not boil. Set it aside to cool. It should be of the consistency of real fresh cream. Serve in a creamer.

STRAWBERRY SPONGE.

One quart of strawberries, half a package of gelatine, one cupful and a half of water, one cupful of sugar, the juice of a lemon, the whites of four eggs. Soak the gelatine for two hours in half a cupful of the water. Mash the strawberries and add half the sugar to them. Boil the remainder of the sugar and the water gently twenty minutes. Rub the strawberries through a sieve. Add the gelatine to the boiling syrup and take from the fire immediately; then add the strawberries. Place in a pan of ice-water and beat five minutes. Add the whites of eggs and beat until the mixture begins to thicken. Pour in the molds and set away to harden. Serve with sugar and cream. Raspberry and blackberry sponges are made in the same way.

LEMON SPONGE.

Lemon sponge is made from the juice of four lemons, four eggs, a cupful of sugar, half a package of gelatine and one pint of water. Strain lemon juice on the sugar; beat the yolks of the eggs and mix with the remainder of the water, having used a half cupful of the pint in which to soak the gelatine. Add the sugar and lemon to this and cook until it begins to thicken, then add the gelatine. Strain this into a basin, which place in a pan of water to cool. Beat with a whisk until it has cooled but not hardened; now add the whites of the eggs until it begins to thicken, turn in a mold and set to harden.

Remember the sponge hardens very rapidly when it commences to cool, so have your molds all ready. Serve with powdered sugar and cream.

APPLE SNOW.

Stew some fine-flavored sour apples tender, sweeten to taste, strain them through a fine wire sieve and break into one pint of strained apples the white of an egg; whisk the apple and egg very briskly till quite stiff and it will be as white as snow; eaten with a nice boiled custard it makes a very desirable dessert. More eggs may be used if liked.

QUINCE SNOW.

Quarter five fair-looking quinces and boil them till they are tender in water, then peel them and push them through a coarse sieve. Sweeten to the taste and add the whites of three or four eggs. Then with an egg-whisk beat all to a stiff froth and pile with a spoon upon a glass dish and set away in the ice box, unless it is to be served immediately.

ORANGE TRIFLE.

Take the thin parings from the outside of a dozen oranges and put to steep in a wide-mouthed bottle; cover it with good cognac and let it stand twenty-four hours; skin and seed the oranges and reduce to a pulp; press this through a sieve, sugar to taste, arrange in a dish and heap with whipped cream flavored with the orange brandy, ice two hours before serving.

LEMON TRIFLE.

The juice of two lemons and grated peel of one, one pint of cream, well sweetened and whipped stiff, one cupful of sherry, a little nutmeg. Let sugar, lemon juice and peel lie together two hours before you add wine and nutmeg. Strain through double tarlatan and whip gradually into the frothed cream. Serve very soon heaped in small glasses. Nice with cake.

FRUIT TRIFLE.

Whites of four eggs beaten to a stiff froth, two tablespoonfuls each of sugar, currant jelly and raspberry jam. Eaten with sponge cakes, it is a delicious dessert.

GRAPE TRIFLE.

Pulp through a sieve two pounds of ripe grapes, enough to keep back the stones, add sugar to taste. Put into a trifle dish and cover > with whipped cream, nicely flavored. Serve very cold.

APPLE TRIFLE.

Peel, core and quarter some good tart apples of nice flavor, and stew them with a strip of orange and a strip of quince peel, sufficient water to cover the bottom of the stewpan, and sugar in the proportion of half a pound to one pound of fruit; when cooked, press the pulp through a sieve, and, when cold, dish and cover with one pint of whipped cream flavored with lemon peel.

Quinces prepared in the same manner are equally as good.

PEACH TRIFLE.

Select perfect, fresh peaches, peel and core and cut in quarters; they should be *well sugared*, arranged in a trifle dish with a few of their own blanched kernels among them, then heaped with whipped cream as above; the cream should not be flavored; this trifle should be set on the ice for at least an hour before serving; home-made sponge cakes should be served with it.

GOOSEBERRY TRIFLE.

One quart of gooseberries, sugar to taste, one pint of custard, a plateful of whipped cream.

Put the gooseberries into a jar, with sufficient moist sugar to sweeten them, and boil them until reduced to a pulp. Put this pulp at the bottom of a trifle dish; pour over it a pint of custard, and, when cold, cover with whipped cream. The cream should be whipped the day before it is wanted for table, as it will then be so much firmer and more solid. This dish may be garnished as fancy dictates.

LEMON HONEY.

One coffeecupful of white sugar, the grated rind and juice of one large lemon, the yolks of three eggs and the white of one, a tablespoonful of butter. Put into a basin the sugar and butter, set it in a dish of boiling water over the fire; while this is melting, beat up the eggs, and add to them the grated rind from the outside of the lemon; then add this to the sugar and butter, cooking and stirring it until it is thick and clear like honey.

This will keep for some days, put into a tight preserve jar, and is nice for flavoring pies, etc.

FLOATING ISLANDS.

Beat the yolks of five eggs and the whites of two very light, sweeten with five tablespoonfuls of sugar and flavor to taste; stir them into a quart of scalded milk and cook it until it thickens. When cool pour it into a glass dish. Now whip the whites of the three remaining eggs to a *stiff* froth, adding three tablespoonfuls of sugar and a little flavoring. Pour this froth over a shallow dish of boiling water; the steam passing through it cooks it; when sufficiently cooked, take a tablespoon and drop spoonfuls of this over the top of the custard, far enough apart so that the "little white islands" will not touch each other. By dropping a teaspoonful of bright jelly on the top or centre of each island, is produced a pleasing effect; also by filling wine-glasses and arranging them around a standard adds much to the appearance of the table.

FLOATING ISLAND.

One quart of milk, five eggs and five tablespoonfuls of sugar. Scald the milk, then add the beaten yolks and one of the whites together with the sugar. First stir into them a little of the scalded milk to prevent curdling, then all of the milk. Cook it the proper thickness; remove from the fire, and, when cool, flavor; then pour it into a glass dish and let it become very cold. Before it is served beat up the remaining four whites of the eggs to a *stiff* froth and beat into them three tablespoonfuls of sugar and two tablespoonfuls of currant jelly. Dip this over the top of the custard.

TAPIOCA BLANC MANGE.

Half a pound of tapioca soaked an hour in one pint of milk and boiled till tender; add a pinch of salt, sweeten to taste and put into a mold; when cold turn it out and serve with strawberry or raspberry jam around it and a little cream. Flavor with lemon or vanilla.

BLANC MANGE. No. 1.

In one teacupful of water boil until dissolved one ounce of clarified isinglass, or of patent gelatine (which is better); stir it continually, while boiling. Then squeeze the juice of a lemon upon a cupful of fine, white sugar; stir the sugar into a quart of rich cream and half a pint of Madeira or sherry wine; when it is well mixed, add the dissolved isinglass or gelatine, stir all well together, pour it into molds previously wet with cold water; set the molds upon ice, let them stand until their contents are hard and cold, then serve with sugar and cream or custard sauce.

BLANC MANGE. No. 2.

Dissolve two ounces of patent gelatine in cold water; when it is dissolved stir it into two quarts of rich milk, with a teacupful of fine white sugar; season it to your taste with lemon, or vanilla, or peach water; place it over the fire and boil it, stirring it continually; let it boil five minutes; then strain it through a cloth, pour it into molds previously wet with cold water and salt; let it stand on ice, or in any cool place until it becomes hard and cold; turn it out carefully upon dishes and serve; or, half fill your mold; when this has set, cover with cherries, peaches in halves, strawberries or sliced bananas, and add the remainder.

CHOCOLATE BLANC MANGE.

Half a box of gelatine soaked in a cupful of water for an hour, half a cupful of grated chocolate, rubbed smooth in a little milk. Boil two cupfuls of milk, then add the gelatine and chocolate and one cupful of sugar; boil all together eight or ten minutes. Remove from the fire, and when nearly cold beat into this the whipped whites of three eggs, flavored with vanilla. Should be served cold with custard made of the yolks, or sugar and cream. Set the molds in a cold place.

CORNSTARCH BLANC MANGE.

Take one quart of sweet milk and put one pint upon the stove to heat; in the other pint mix four heaping tablespoonfuls of cornstarch and half a cupful of sugar; when the milk is hot, pour in the cold milk with the cornstarch and sugar thoroughly mixed in it and stir altogether until there are no lumps and it is thick; flavor with lemon; take from the stove and add the whites of three eggs beaten to a stiff froth.

A Custard for the above.—One pint of milk boiled with a little salt in it; beat the yolks of three eggs with half a cupful of sugar and add to the boiling milk; stir well, but do not let it boil until the eggs are put in; flavor to taste.

FRUIT BLANC MANGE.

Stew nice, fresh fruit (cherries, raspberries and strawberries being the best), or canned ones will do; strain off the juice and sweeten to taste; place it over the fire in a double kettle until it boils; while boiling, stir in cornstarch wet with a little cold water, allowing two tablespoonfuls of cornstarch to each pint of juice; continue stirring until sufficiently cooked; then pour into molds wet in cold water and set away to cool. Served with cream and sugar.

ORANGE CHARLOTTE.

For two molds of medium size, soak half a box of gelatine in half a cupful of water for two hours. Add one and a half cupfuls of boiling water and strain. Then add two cupfuls of sugar, one of orange juice and pulp and the juice of one lemon. Stir until the mixture begins to cool, or about five minutes; then add the whites of six eggs, beaten to a stiff froth. Beat the whole until so stiff that it will only just pour into molds lined with sections of orange. Set away to cool.

STRAWBERRY CHARLOTTE.

Make a boiled custard of one quart of milk, the yolks of six eggs and three-quarters of a cupful of sugar; flavor to taste. Line a glass fruit-dish with slices of sponge cake dipped in sweet cream; lay upon this ripe strawberries sweetened to taste; then a layer of cake and strawberries as before. When the custard is cold pour over the whole. Now beat the whites of the eggs to a stiff froth, add a tablespoonful of sugar to each egg and put over the top. Decorate the top with the largest berries saved out at the commencement.

Raspberry charlotte may be made the same way.

CHARLOTTE RUSSE. (Fine.)

Whip one quart of rich cream to a stiff froth and drain well on a nice sieve. To one scant pint of milk add six eggs beaten very light; make very sweet; flavor high with vanilla. Cook over hot water till it is a thick custard. Soak one full ounce of Cox's gelatine in a very little water and warm over hot water. When the custard is very cold beat in lightly the gelatine and the whipped cream. Line the bottom of your mold with buttered paper, the side with sponge cake or lady-fingers fastened together with the white of an egg. Fill with the cream, put in a cold place, or, in summer, on ice. To turn out, dip the mold for a moment in hot water. In draining the whipped cream, all that drips through can be re-whipped.

CHARLOTTE RUSSE.

Cut stale sponge cake into slices about half an inch thick and line three molds with them, leaving a space of half an inch between each slice; set the molds where they will not be disturbed until the filling is ready. Take a deep tin pan and fill about one-third full of either snow or pounded ice and into this set another pan that will hold at least four quarts. Into a deep bowl or pail (a whip churn is better) put one and a half pints of cream (if the cream is very thick take one pint of cream and a half pint of milk); whip it to a froth and when the bowl is full, skim the froth into the pan which is standing on the ice and repeat this until the cream is all froth; then with a spoon draw the froth to one side and you will find that some of the cream has gone back to milk; turn this into the bowl again and whip as before; when the cream is all whipped, stir into it two-thirds of a cup of powdered sugar, one teaspoonful of vanilla and half of a box of gelatine, which has been soaked in cold water enough to cover it for one hour and then put in boiling water enough to dissolve it (about half a cup); stir from the bottom of the pan until it begins to grow stiff; fill the molds and set them on ice in the pan for one hour, or until they are sent to the table. When ready to dish them, loosen lightly at the sides and turn out on a flat dish. Have the cream ice cold when you begin to whip it; and it is a good plan to put a lump of ice into the cream while whipping it.

ANOTHER CHARLOTTE RUSSE.

Two tablespoonfuls of gelatine soaked in a little cold milk two hours, two coffeecupfuls of rich cream, one teacupful of milk. Whip the cream stiff in a large bowl or dish; set on ice. Boil the milk and pour gradually over the gelatine until dissolved, then strain; when nearly cold, add the whipped cream, a spoonful at a time. Sweeten with powdered sugar, flavor with extract of vanilla. Line a dish with lady-fingers or sponge cake; pour in cream and set in a cool place to harden. This is about the same recipe as M. Parloa's, but is not as explicit in detail.

PLAIN CHARLOTTE RUSSE. No. 1.

Make a rule of white sponge cake; bake in narrow shallow pans. Then make a custard of the yolks after this recipe. Wet a saucepan with cold water to prevent the milk that will be scalded in it from burning. Pour out the water and put in a quart of milk, boil and partly cool. Beat up the yolks of six eggs and add three ounces of sugar and a saltspoonful of salt; mix thoroughly and add the lukewarm milk. Stir and pour the custard into a porcelain or double saucepan and stir while on the range until of the consistency of cream; do not allow it to boil, as that would curdle it; strain, and when almost cold add two teaspoonfuls of vanilla. Now, having arranged your cake (cut into inch slices) around the sides and on the bottom of a glass dish, pour over the custard. If you wish a meringue on the top, beat up the whites of four eggs with four tablespoonfuls of sugar; flavor with lemon or vanilla, spread over the top and brown slightly in the oven.

PLAIN CHARLOTTE RUSSE. No. 2.

Put some thin slices of sponge cake in the bottom of a glass sauce dish; pour in wine enough to soak it; beat up the whites of three eggs until very light; add to it three tablespoonfuls of finely powdered sugar, a glass of sweet wine and one pint of thick sweet cream; beat it well and pour over the cake. Set it in a cold place until served.

NAPLE BISCUITS, OR CHARLOTTE RUSSE.

Make a double rule of sponge cake; bake it in round deep patty-pans; when cold cut out the inside about one-quarter of an inch from the edge and bottom, leaving the shell. Replace the inside with a custard made of the yolks of four eggs beaten with a pint of boiling milk, sweetened and flavored; lay on the top of this some jelly or jam; beat the whites of three eggs with three heaping tablespoonfuls of powdered sugar until it will stand in a heap; flavor it a little; place this on the jelly. Set them aside in a cold place until time to serve.

ECONOMICAL CHARLOTTE RUSSE.

Make a quart of nicely flavored mock custard, put it into a large glass fruit dish, which is partly filled with stale cake (of any kind) cut up into small pieces about an inch square, stir it a little, then beat the whites of two or more eggs stiff, sweetened with white sugar; spread over the top, set in a refrigerator to become cold.

Or, to be still more economical: To make the cream, take a pint and a half of milk, set it on the stove to boil; mix together in a bowl the following named articles: large half cup of sugar, one moderately heaped teaspoonful of cornstarch, two tablespoonfuls of grated chocolate one egg, a small half cup of milk and a pinch of salt. Pour into the boiling milk, remove to top of the stove and let simmer a minute or two. When the cream is cold pour over the cake just before setting it on the table. Serve in saucers. If you do not have plenty of eggs you can use all cornstarch, about two heaping teaspoonfuls; but be careful and not get the cream too thick, and have it free from lumps.

The cream should be flavored either with vanilla or lemon extract. Nutmeg might answer.

TIPSY CHARLOTTE.

Take a stale sponge cake, cut the bottom and sides of it, so as to make it stand even in a glass fruit dish; make a few deep gashes through it with a sharp knife, pour over it a pint of good wine, let it stand and soak into the cake. In the meantime, blanch, peel and slice lengthwise half a pound of sweet almonds; stick them all over the top of the cake. Have ready a pint of good boiled custard, well flavored, and pour over the whole. To be dished with a spoon. This is equally as good as any charlotte.

ORANGE CHARLOTTE.

One-third of a box of gelatine, one-third of a cupful of cold water, one-third of a cupful of boiling water and one cup of sugar, the juice of one lemon and one cupful of orange juice and pulp, a little grated orange peel and the whites of four eggs. Soak the gelatine in the cold water one hour. Pour the boiling water over the lemon and orange juice, cover it and let stand half an hour; then add the sugar, let it come to a boil on the fire, stir in the gelatine and when it is thoroughly dissolved, take from the fire. When cool enough, beat into it the four beaten whites of eggs, turn into the mold and set in a cold place to stiffen, first placing pieces of sponge cake all around the mold.

BURNT ALMOND CHARLOTTE.

One cupful of sweet almonds, blanched and chopped fine, half a box of gelatine soaked two hours in half a cupful of cold water; when the gelatine is sufficiently soaked, put three tablespoonfuls of sugar into a saucepan over the fire and stir until it becomes liquid and looks dark; then add the chopped almonds to it and stir two minutes more; turn it out on a platter and set aside to get cool. After they become cool enough break them up in a mortar, put them in a cup and a half of milk, and cook again for ten minutes. Now beat together the yolks of two eggs with a cupful of sugar, and add to the cooking mixture; add also the gelatine; stir until smooth and well dissolved; take from the fire and set in a basin of ice-water and beat it until it begins to thicken; then add to that two quarts of whipped cream, and turn the whole carefully into molds, set away on the ice to become firm. Sponge cake can be placed around the mold or not, as desired.

CHARLOTTE RUSSE, WITH PINEAPPLE.

Peel and cut a pineapple in slices, put the slices into a stewpan with half a pound of fine white sugar, half an ounce of isinglass, or of patent gelatine (which is better), and half a teacupful of water; stew it until it is quite tender, then rub it through a sieve, place it upon ice, and stir it well; when it is upon the point of setting, add a pint of cream well whipped, mix it well and pour it into a mold lined with sponge cake, or prepared in any other way you prefer.

COUNTRY PLUM CHARLOTTE.

Stone a quart of ripe plums; first stew and then sweeten them. Cut slices of bread and butter and lay them in the bottom and around the sides of a large bowl or deep dish. Pour in the plums boiling hot, cover the bowl and set it away to cool gradually. When quite cool, send it to the table and eat it with cream.

VELVET CREAM, WITH STRAWBERRIES.

Dissolve half an ounce of gelatine in a gill of water; add to it half a pint of light sherry, grated lemon peel and the juice of one lemon and five ounces of sugar. Stir over the fire until the sugar is thoroughly dissolved. Then strain and cool. Before it sets beat into it a pint of cream; pour into molds and keep on ice until wanted. Half fill the small molds with fine strawberries, pour the mixture on top, and place on ice until wanted.

CORNSTARCH MERINGUE.

Heat a quart of milk until it boils, add four heaping teaspoonfuls of cornstarch which has previously been dissolved in a little cold milk. Stir constantly while boiling for fifteen minutes. Remove from the fire, and gradually add while hot the yolks of five eggs, beaten together with three-fourths of a cupful of sugar, and flavored with lemon, vanilla or bitter almond. Bake this mixture for fifteen minutes in a well-buttered pudding-dish or until it begins to "set."

Make a meringue of the whites of five eggs, whipped stiff with a half cupful of jelly, and spread evenly over the custard, without removing the same farther than the edge of the oven.

Use currant jelly if vanilla is used in the custard, crab apple for bitter almond and strawberry for lemon. Cover and bake for five minutes, after which take off the lid and brown the meringue a very little. Sift powdered sugar thickly over the top. To be eaten cold.

WASHINGTON PIE.

This recipe is the same as "Boston Cream Pie" (adding half an ounce of butter), which may be found under the head of PASTRY, PIES AND TARTS. In summer time, it is a good plan to bake the pie the day before wanted; then when cool, wrap around it a paper and place it in the ice box so to have it get *very cold*; then serve it with a dish of fresh strawberries or raspberries. A delicious dessert.

CREAM PIE.

Make two cakes as for Washington pie, then take one cup of sweet cream and three tablespoonfuls of white sugar. Beat with egg-beater or fork till it is stiff enough to put on without running off and flavor with vanilla. If you beat it after it is stiff it will come to butter. Put between the cakes and on top.

DESSERT PUFFS.

Puffs for dessert are delicate and nice; take one pint of milk and cream each, the whites of four eggs beaten to a stiff froth, one heaping cupful of sifted flour, one scant cupful of powdered sugar, add a little grated lemon peel and a little salt; beat these all together till very light, bake in gem-pans, sift pulverized sugar over them and eat with sauce flavored with lemon.

PEACH CAKE FOR DESSERT.

Bake three sheets of sponge cake, as for jelly cake; cut nice ripe peaches in thin slices, or chop them; prepare cream by whipping, sweetening and adding flavor of vanilla, if desired; put layers of peaches between the sheets of cake; pour cream over each layer and over the top. To be eaten soon after it is prepared.

FRUIT SHORT-CAKES.

For the recipes of strawberry, peach and other fruit short-cakes, look under the head of BISCUITS, ROLLS AND MUFFINS. They all make a very delicious dessert when served with a pitcher of fresh sweet cream, when obtainable.

SALTED OR ROASTED ALMONDS.

Blanch half a pound of almonds. Put with them a tablespoonful of melted butter and one of salt. Stir them till well mixed, then spread them over a baking-pan and bake fifteen minutes, or till crisp, stirring often. They must be bright yellow-brown when done. They are a fashionable appetizer and should be placed in ornamental dishes at the beginning of dinner, and are used by some in place of olives, which, however, should also be on the table, or some fine pickles may take their place.

ROAST CHESTNUTS.

Peel the raw chestnuts and scald them to remove the inner skin; put them in a frying pan with a little butter and toss them about a few moments; add a sprinkle of salt and a suspicion of cayenne. Serve them after the cheese.

Peanuts may be blanched and roasted the same.

AFTER-DINNER CROUTONS.

These crispy *croutons* answer as a substitute for hard-water crackers and are also relished by most people.

Cut sandwich bread into slices one-quarter of an inch thick; cut each slice into four small triangles; dry them in the oven slowly until they assume a delicate brownish tint, then serve either hot or cold. A nice way to serve them is to spread a paste of part butter and part rich creamy cheese, to which may be added a very little minced parsley.

ORANGE FLOAT.

To make orange float, take one quart of water, the juice and pulp of two lemons, one coffeecupful of sugar. When boiling hot, add four tablespoonfuls of cornstarch. Let it boil fifteen minutes, stirring all the time. When cold, pour it over four or five oranges that have been sliced into a glass dish and over the top spread the beaten whites of three eggs, sweetened and flavored with vanilla. A nice dessert.

LEMON TOAST.

This dessert can be made very conveniently without much preparation.

Take the yolks of six eggs, beat them well and add three cupfuls of sweet milk; take baker's bread, not too stale, and cut into slices; dip them into the milk and eggs and lay the slices into a spider, with sufficient melted butter, hot, to fry a delicate brown. Take the whites of the six eggs and beat them to a froth, adding a large cupful of white sugar; add the juice of two lemons, heating well and adding two cupfuls of boiling water. Serve over the toast as a sauce and you will find it a very delicious dish.

SWEET OMELET. No. 1.

One tablespoonful of butter, two of sugar, one cupful of milk, four eggs. Let the milk come to a boil. Beat the flour and butter together; add to them gradually the boiling milk and cook eight minutes; stirring often; beat the sugar and the yolks of the eggs together; add to the cooked mixture and set away to cool. When cool, beat the whites of the eggs to a stiff froth and add to the mixture. Bake in a buttered pudding-dish for twenty minutes in a moderate oven. Serve *immediately* with creamy sauce.

SWEET OMELET. No. 2.

Four eggs, two tablespoonfuls of sugar, a pinch of salt, half a teaspoonful of vanilla extract, one cupful of whipped cream. Beat the whites of the eggs to a stiff froth and gradually beat the flavoring and sugar into them. When well beaten add the yolks and, lastly, the whipped cream. Have a dish holding about one quart slightly buttered. Pour the mixture into this and bake just twelve minutes. Serve the moment it is taken from the oven.

SALAD OF MIXED FRUITS.

Put in the centre of a dish a pineapple properly pared, cored and sliced, yet retaining as near as practicable its original shape. Peel, quarter and remove the seeds from four sweet oranges; arrange them in a border around the pineapple. Select four fine bananas, peel and cut into slices lengthwise; arrange these zigzag-fence fashion around the border of the dish. In the V-shaped spaces around the dish put tiny mounds of grapes of mixed colors. When complete, the dish should look very appetizing. To half a pint of clear sugar syrup add half an ounce of good brandy, pour over the fruit and serve.

ORANGE COCOANUT SALAD.

Peel and slice a dozen oranges, grate a cocoanut and slice a pineapple. Put alternate layers of each until the dish is full. Then pour over them sweetened wine. Served with small cakes.

When oranges are served whole, they should be peeled and prettily arranged in a fruit dish. A small knife is best for this purpose. Break the skin from the stem into six or eight even parts, peel each section down half way, and tuck the point in next to the orange.

CRYSTALLIZED FRUIT.

Pick out the finest of any kind of fruit, leave on their stalks, beat the whites of three eggs to a stiff froth, lay the fruit in the beaten egg with the stalks upward, drain them and beat the part that drips off again; select them out, one by one and dip them into a cup of finely powdered sugar; cover a pan with a sheet of fine paper, place the fruit inside of it, and put it in an oven that is cooling; when the icing on the fruit becomes firm, pile them on a dish and set them in a cool place. For this purpose, oranges or lemons should be carefully pared, and all the white inner skin removed that is possible, to prevent bitterness; then cut either in thin horizontal slices if lemons, or in quarters if oranges. For cherries, strawberries, currants, etc., choose the largest and finest, leaving stems out. Peaches should be pared and cut in halves and sweet juicy pears may be treated in the same way, or look nicely when pared, leaving on the stems and iced. Pineapples should be cut in thin slices and these again divided into quarters.

PEACHES AND CREAM.

Pare and slice the peaches just before sending to table. Cover the glass dish containing them to exclude the air as much as possible, as they soon change color. Do not sugar them in the dish—they then become preserves, not fresh fruit. Pass the powdered sugar and cream with them.

SNOW PYRAMID.

Beat to a stiff foam the whites of half a dozen eggs, add a small teacupful of currant jelly and whip all together again. Fill half full of cream as many saucers as you have guests, dropping in the centre of each saucer a tablespoonful of the beaten eggs and jelly in the shape of a pyramid.

JELLY FRITTERS.

Make a batter of three eggs, a pint of milk and a pint bowl of wheat flour or more, beat it light; put a tablespoonful of lard or beef fat in a frying or omelet pan, add a saltspoonful of salt, making it boiling hot, put in the batter by the large spoonful, not too close; when one side is a delicate brown, turn the other; when done, take them on to a dish with a d'oyley over it; put a dessertspoonful of firm jelly or jam on each and serve. A very nice dessert.

STEWED APPLES. No. 1.

Take a dozen green tart apples, core and slice them, put into a saucepan with just enough water to cover them, cover the saucepan closely, and stew the apples until they are tender and clear; then take them out, put them into a deep dish and cover them; add to the juice in the saucepan a cupful of loaf sugar for every twelve apples, and boil it half an hour, adding to the syrup a pinch of mace and a dozen whole cloves just ten minutes before taking from the fire; pour scalding hot over the apples and set them in a cold place; eat ice cold with cream or boiled custard.

STEWED APPLES. No. 2.

Apples cooked in the following way look very pretty on a tea-table and are appreciated by the palate. Select firm round greenings, pare neatly and cut in halves; place in a shallow stewpan with sufficient boiling water to cover them and a cup of sugar to every six apples. Each half should cook on the bottom of the pan and be removed from the others so as not to injure its shape. Stew slowly until the pieces are very tender; remove to a glass dish carefully, boil the syrup a half hour longer, pour it over the apples and eat cold. A few pieces of lemon boiled in the syrup add to the flavor.

BAKED PEARS.

Pare and core the pears without dividing; place them in a pan and fill up the orifice with brown sugar; add a little water and let them bake until perfectly tender. Nice with sweet cream or boiled custard.

STEWED PEARS.

Stewed pears with a thick syrup make a fine dessert dish accompanied with cake.

Peel and cut them in halves, leaving the stems on and scoop out the cores. Put them into a saucepan, placing them close together, with the stems uppermost. Pour over sufficient water, a cup of sugar, a few whole cloves and some sticks of cinnamon, a tablespoonful of lemon juice. Cover the stewpan closely, to stew gently till the fruit is done, which will depend on the quality of the fruit. Then take out the fruit carefully and arrange it on a dish for serving. Boil down the syrup until quite thick; strain it and allow it to cool enough to set it; then pour it over the fruit.

The juice could be colored by a few drops of liquid cochineal, or a few slices of beets, while boiling. A teaspoonful of brandy adds much to the flavor. Serve with cream or boiled custard.

BAKED QUINCES.

Take ripe quinces, pare and quarter them, cut out the seeds; then stew them in clear water until a straw will pierce them; put into a baking dish with half a cupful of loaf sugar to every eight quinces; pour over them the liquor in which they were boiled, cover closely and bake in the oven one hour; then take out the quinces and put them into a covered dish; return the syrup to the saucepan and boil twenty minutes; then pour over the quinces and set them away to cool.

GOOSEBERRY FOOL.

Stew a quart of ripe gooseberries in just enough water to cover them; when soft, rub them through a colander to remove the skins and seeds; while hot stir into them a tablespoonful of melted butter and a cupful of sugar. Beat the yolks of three eggs and add that; whip all together until light. Fill a large glass fruit dish and spread on the top the beaten whites mixed with three tablespoonfuls of sugar. Apples or any tart fruit is nice made in this manner.

MERINGUES OR KISSES.

A coffeecupful of fine white sugar, the whites of six eggs; whisk the whites of the eggs to a stiff froth and with a wooden spoon stir in *quickly* the pounded sugar; and have some boards put in the oven thick enough to prevent the bottom of the meringues from acquiring too much color. Cut some strips of paper about two inches wide; place this paper on the board and drop a tablespoonful at a time of the mixture on the paper, taking care to let all the meringues be the same size. In dropping it from the spoon, give the mixture the form of an egg and keep the meringues about two inches apart from each other on the paper. Strew over them some sifted sugar and bake in a moderate oven for half an hour. As soon as they begin to color, remove them from the oven; take each slip of paper by the two ends and turn it gently on the table and with a small spoon take out the soft part of each meringue. Spread some clean paper on the board, turn the meringues upside down and put them into the oven to harden and brown on the other side. When required for table, fill them with whipped cream, flavored with liquor or vanilla and sweeten with pounded sugar. Join two of the meringues together and pile them high in the dish. To vary their appearance, finely chopped almonds or currants may be strewn over them before the sugar is sprinkled over; and they may be garnished with any bright-colored preserve. Great expedition is necessary in making this sweet dish, as, if the meringues are not put into the oven as soon as the sugar and eggs are mixed, the former melts and the mixture would run on the paper instead of keeping its egg-shape. The sweeter the meringues are made the crisper will they be; but if there is not sufficient sugar mixed with them, they will most likely be tough. They are sometimes colored with cochineal; and if kept well-covered in a dry place, will remain good for a month or six weeks.

JELLY KISSES.

Kisses, to be served for dessert at a large dinner, with other suitable confectionery, may be varied in this way: Having made the kisses, heap them in the shape of half an egg, placed upon stiff letter paper lining the bottom of a thick baking pan; put them in a moderate oven until the outside is a little hardened; then take one off carefully, take out the soft inside with the handle of a spoon, and put it back with the mixture, to make more; then lay the shell down. Take another and prepare it likewise; fill the shells with currant jelly or jam; join two together, cementing them with some of the mixture; so continue until you have enough. Make kisses, cocoanut drops, and such like, the day before they are wanted.

This recipe will make a fair-sized cake basket full. It adds much to their beauty when served up to tint half of them pale pink, then unite white and pink. Serve on a high glass dish.

COCOANUT MACAROONS.

Make a "kiss" mixture, add to it the white meat, grated, and finish as directed for KISSES.

ALMOND MACAROONS.

Half a pound of sweet almonds, a coffeecupful of white sugar, the whites of two eggs; blanch the almonds and pound them to a paste; add to them the sugar and the beaten whites of eggs; work the whole together with the back of a spoon, then roll the mixture in your hands in balls about the size of a nutmeg, dust sugar over the top, lay them on a sheet of paper at least an inch apart. Bake in a cool oven a light brown.

CHOCOLATE MACAROONS.

Put three ounces of plain chocolate in a pan and melt on a slow fire; then work it to a thick paste with one pound of powdered sugar and the whites of three eggs; roll the mixture down to the thickness of about one-quarter of an inch; cut it in small, round pieces with a paste-cutter, either plain or scalloped; butter a pan slightly, and dust it with flour and sugar in equal quantities; place in it the pieces of paste or mixture, and bake in a hot but not too quick oven.

www.ingramcontent.com/pod-product-compliance
Lightning Source LLC
Chambersburg PA
CBHW081624100526
44590CB00021B/3589